Two letters of Sir Isaac Newton to Mr. Le Clerc, ... in Holland. The former containing a dissertation upon ... I John, v.7. The latter upon ... I Timothy, iii. 16. Published from authentick MSS ...

Isaac Newton

Two letters of Sir Isaac Newton to Mr. Le Clerc, ... in Holland. The former containing a dissertation upon ... I John, v.7. The latter upon ... I Timothy, iii. 16. Published from authentick MSS ...
Newton, Isaac, Sir
ESTCID: T018648
Reproduction from British Library
With a half-title.
London : printed for J. Payne, 1754.
[4],123,[1]p. ; 8°

ECCO
Eighteenth Century
Collections Online
Print Editions

Gale ECCO Print Editions

Relive history with *Eighteenth Century Collections Online*, now available in print for the independent historian and collector. This series includes the most significant English-language and foreign-language works printed in Great Britain during the eighteenth century, and is organized in seven different subject areas including literature and language; medicine, science, and technology; and religion and philosophy. The collection also includes thousands of important works from the Americas.

The eighteenth century has been called "The Age of Enlightenment." It was a period of rapid advance in print culture and publishing, in world exploration, and in the rapid growth of science and technology – all of which had a profound impact on the political and cultural landscape. At the end of the century the American Revolution, French Revolution and Industrial Revolution, perhaps three of the most significant events in modern history, set in motion developments that eventually dominated world political, economic, and social life.

In a groundbreaking effort, Gale initiated a revolution of its own: digitization of epic proportions to preserve these invaluable works in the largest online archive of its kind. Contributions from major world libraries constitute over 175,000 original printed works. Scanned images of the actual pages, rather than transcriptions, recreate the works *as they first appeared.*

Now for the first time, these high-quality digital scans of original works are available via print-on-demand, making them readily accessible to libraries, students, independent scholars, and readers of all ages.

For our initial release we have created seven robust collections to form one the world's most comprehensive catalogs of 18th century works.

Initial Gale ECCO Print Editions collections include:

> *History and Geography*
> Rich in titles on English life and social history, this collection spans the world as it was known to eighteenth-century historians and explorers. Titles include a wealth of travel accounts and diaries, histories of nations from throughout the world, and maps and charts of a world that was still being discovered. Students of the War of American Independence will find fascinating accounts from the British side of conflict.

Social Science
Delve into what it was like to live during the eighteenth century by reading the first-hand accounts of everyday people, including city dwellers and farmers, businessmen and bankers, artisans and merchants, artists and their patrons, politicians and their constituents. Original texts make the American, French, and Industrial revolutions vividly contemporary.

Medicine, Science and Technology
Medical theory and practice of the 1700s developed rapidly, as is evidenced by the extensive collection, which includes descriptions of diseases, their conditions, and treatments. Books on science and technology, agriculture, military technology, natural philosophy, even cookbooks, are all contained here.

Literature and Language
Western literary study flows out of eighteenth-century works by Alexander Pope, Daniel Defoe, Henry Fielding, Frances Burney, Denis Diderot, Johann Gottfried Herder, Johann Wolfgang von Goethe, and others. Experience the birth of the modern novel, or compare the development of language using dictionaries and grammar discourses.

Religion and Philosophy
The Age of Enlightenment profoundly enriched religious and philosophical understanding and continues to influence present-day thinking. Works collected here include masterpieces by David Hume, Immanuel Kant, and Jean-Jacques Rousseau, as well as religious sermons and moral debates on the issues of the day, such as the slave trade. The Age of Reason saw conflict between Protestantism and Catholicism transformed into one between faith and logic -- a debate that continues in the twenty-first century.

Law and Reference
This collection reveals the history of English common law and Empire law in a vastly changing world of British expansion. Dominating the legal field is the *Commentaries of the Law of England* by Sir William Blackstone, which first appeared in 1765. Reference works such as almanacs and catalogues continue to educate us by revealing the day-to-day workings of society.

Fine Arts
The eighteenth-century fascination with Greek and Roman antiquity followed the systematic excavation of the ruins at Pompeii and Herculaneum in southern Italy; and after 1750 a neoclassical style dominated all artistic fields. The titles here trace developments in mostly English-language works on painting, sculpture, architecture, music, theater, and other disciplines. Instructional works on musical instruments, catalogs of art objects, comic operas, and more are also included.

bibliolife
old books, new life.

The BiblioLife Network

This project was made possible in part by the BiblioLife Network (BLN), a project aimed at addressing some of the huge challenges facing book preservationists around the world. The BLN includes libraries, library networks, archives, subject matter experts, online communities and library service providers. We believe every book ever published should be available as a high-quality print reproduction; printed on-demand anywhere in the world. This insures the ongoing accessibility of the content and helps generate sustainable revenue for the libraries and organizations that work to preserve these important materials.

The following book is in the "public domain" and represents an authentic reproduction of the text as printed by the original publisher. While we have attempted to accurately maintain the integrity of the original work, there are sometimes problems with the original work or the micro-film from which the books were digitized. This can result in minor errors in reproduction. Possible imperfections include missing and blurred pages, poor pictures, markings and other reproduction issues beyond our control. Because this work is culturally important, we have made it available as part of our commitment to protecting, preserving, and promoting the world's literature.

GUIDE TO FOLD-OUTS MAPS and OVERSIZED IMAGES

The book you are reading was digitized from microfilm captured over the past thirty to forty years. Years after the creation of the original microfilm, the book was converted to digital files and made available in an online database.

In an online database, page images do not need to conform to the size restrictions found in a printed book. When converting these images back into a printed bound book, the page sizes are standardized in ways that maintain the detail of the original. For large images, such as fold-out maps, the original page image is split into two or more pages

Guidelines used to determine how to split the page image follows:

- Some images are split vertically; large images require vertical and horizontal splits.
- For horizontal splits, the content is split left to right.
- For vertical splits, the content is split from top to bottom.
- For both vertical and horizontal splits, the image is processed from top left to bottom right.

TWO LETTERS

OF

Sir *ISAAC NEWTON*

TO

Mr. *LE CLERC*,

Late Divinity Professor of the REMONSTRANTS in *HOLLAND*.

TWO LETTERS

OF

Sir *ISAAC NEWTON*

TO

Mr. *LE CLERC*,

Late Divinity Professor of the REMONSTRANTS in *HOLLAND*.

The FORMER

Containing a DISSERTATION upon the Reading of the Greek Text, 1 JOHN, v. 7.

The LATTER

Upon That of 1 TIMOTHY, iii. 16.

Published from authentick MSS in the Library of the REMONSTRANTS in *HOLLAND*.

LONDON:

Printed for J. PAYNE, at POPE's HEAD in PATER-NOSTER-ROW.

MDCCLIV.

FIRST LETTER:

CONTAINING,

A DISSERTATION upon the following Passage in the First Epistle of St. John.

CHAP. V. Ver. 6, 7, 8, 9.

Verse 6. Οὗτός ἐστιν ὁ ἐλθὼν δι' ὕδατος καὶ αἵματος, Ἰησοῦς ὁ Χριστός· οὐκ ἐν τῷ ὕδατι μόνον, ἀλλ' ἐν τῷ ὕδατι καὶ τῷ αἵματι· καὶ τὸ πνεῦμά ἐστι τὸ μαρτυροῦν, ὅτι τὸ πνεῦμά ἐστιν ἡ ἀλήθεια·

Verse 7. Ὅτι τρεῖς εἰσιν οἱ μαρτυροῦντες ΕΝ ΤΩ ΟΥΡΑΝΩ, Ο ΠΑΤΗΡ, Ο ΛΟΓΟΣ, ΚΑΙ ΤΟ ΑΓΙΟΝ ΠΝΕΥΜΑ· ΚΑΙ ΟΥΤΟΙ ΟΙ ΤΡΕΙΣ ΕΝ ΕΙΣΙ.

Verse 8. ΚΑΙ ΤΡΕΙΣ ΕΙΣΙΝ ΟΙ ΜΑΡΤΥΡΟΥΝΤΕΣ ΕΝ ΤΗ ΓΗ, τὸ πνεῦμά, καὶ τὸ ὕδωρ, καὶ τὸ αἷμα· καὶ οἱ τρεῖς εἰς τὸ ἕν εἰσιν.

Verse 9. Εἰ τὴν μαρτυρίαν τῶν ἀνθρώπων λαμβάνομεν, ἡ μαρτυρία τῦ Θεῦ μείζων ἐστίν.

B   English

English Version.

I. Epist. John, Chap. V. Verses 6, 7, 8, 9.

Verse 6. " This is he that came by Wa-
" ter and Blood, *even* Jesus Christ; not by
" Water only; but Water and Blood; and
" it is the Spirit that beareth witness, because
" the Spirit is truth.

Verse 7. " For there are Three that bear
" record IN HEAVEN, THE FATHER, THE
" WORD, AND THE HOLY GHOST: AND
" THESE THREE ARE ONE.

Verse 8. " AND THERE ARE THREE
" THAT BEAR WITNESS IN EARTH, the
" Spirit, and the Water, and the Blood;
" and these Three agree in One.

Verse 9. " If we receive the witness of
" men, the witness of God is greater: &c."

SIR,

SIR,

HOW it has come to pass, that all the printed Greek, as well as Latin editions of the New Testament in use, should agree in giving us the present reading of the Sixth, Seventh and Eighth Verses of the Fifth Chapter of the First Epistle of Saint JOHN, will be matter of surprise to, and raise the curiosity of every person, who is much conversant in the Antiquities of the Christian Church. For all the late printed Greek and Latin Books do now constantly read.

read. " It is the Spirit, that beareth wit-
" ness, because the Spirit is truth. For
" there are Three, that bear record IN
" HEAVEN; THE FATHER, THE WORD,
" AND THE HOLY GHOST: AND THESE
" THREE ARE ONE. AND THERE ARE
" THREE, THAT BEAR WITNESS IN EARTH,
" the Spirit, and the Water, and the Blood:
" and these Three agree in One." Whereas all the Greek Manuscripts of the New Testament, and all the ancient Versions, that have been made of it into any Language whatever, (if we except the vulgar Latin, and it can be fully proved, that this did also accord with all the other versions, till it was reformed and corrected by Jerome) are quite silent in regard to the testimony of " the Three in Heaven", and all the councils, fathers, commentators and other writers, at least of the four first centuries of the Church, as often as in any of their writings they were led to consider the passage before us, do plainly shew, that it stood in their books, " It is the Spirit that
" beareth witness; because the Spirit is
" Truth: For there are Three that bear
" record, the Spirit, the Water and the
" Blood. and these Three agree in One."

. And

And that this Testimony of "the Three in Heaven", was neither in the ancient Greek manuscripts, nor in the early versions; but wholly unknown to the first ages of the Church, may reasonably be presumed from this circumstance alone, that in all that warm, universal and lasting controversy about the Trinity, which began long before, and continued long after Jerome's time, we do not find any one of the writers on the side of the Trinity making the least use of this testimony; even while they industriously ransacked both the Old and New Testament in search after, and in their disputes actually produced every text, allusion or distant hint therein found, that with the least shadow of probability could be of service in their cause. Is it then probable, if their books read, as ours do at this time, that no one of the disputants should hit upon a passage, that stands so very fair to their purpose as the testimony of "the Three in Heaven", most evidently does?

It has indeed been insisted, that in the writings of Cyprian, an eminent Father, about the middle of the third Century, there are two passages, which must suppose him to have the same reading before him,

as in our printed books. The learned Editor of his works, in anfwer to a charge brought againſt Jerome for being a falſary, and the firſt author of this interpolation, remarks,* " That it is a fufficient confuta-
" tion of this very heavy calumny brought
" againſt St. Jerome, that Cyprian has
" quoted it [' the teſtimony of the Three in
" Heaven',] who wrote not only before
" the time of Jerome, but even that of
" Arius, and before the commencement of
" the long controverſy about the Trinity."
I wonder much to find it here affirmed, that Cyprian has quoted the teſtimony of " the Three in Heaven"; all that can poſſibly be imagined is, that he had it in his thoughts at thoſe times, and if I am not very much miſtaken, it was not even there. For a fufficient account may be given of his

---

" * Cui graviſſimæ calumniæ de D Hieronimo
" falſario, et S Scripturarum interpolatore amoliendæ
" ſufficere poterit, Cyprianum citaſſe (nempe triplex
" teſtimonium Patris, Verbi et Spiritus Sancti in cœlo
" teſtantium, non modo ante Hieronimi tempora, ſed
" Arianos, et litem de dogmate illo de trino et uno
" Deo, ſcriptorem. qui tamen hic loci, et in epiſtola
" Jubaiorum hanc pericope agnoſcit."—*Not. Pearſoni,*
Cyप्रiani Tractat. de Unit. Eccleſiæ, p. 109

words,

words, without supposing him to have such a reading in his books. In one of the passages referred to, Cyprian, in proving the Unity of the Church, argues thus.† "The "Lord says, (JOHN X. 20.) *I and the* "*Father are One*. and again it is written "of the Father and the Son and the Holy "Ghost. *And these Three are One.* [One "Thing]. And does any Man believe, "that this Unity proceeding from the "divine firmness, and cohering in the "heavenly misteries, can be cut asunder in "the Church, and parted by the separation "of contradictory wills?"---In the other passage disputing the validity of the baptism of hereticks supposed to deny one or other of the Persons in the Trinity, he reasons thus. "If a person can be baptised "by them, he can obtain pardon of his "sins; and if he can obtain pardon of his

---

" † Dicit Dominus, *Ego et Pater Unum sumus.* Et
" iterum, de Patre, et Filio, et Spiritu Sancto scriptum
" est *Et hi Tres Unum sunt* Et quisquam credit
" hanc unitatem de divina firmitate venientem, sacra-
" mentis cœlestibus cohærentem, scindi in ecclesiâ
" posse, aut voluntatum collidentium divortio separari?"
—*Cyprian. Tractat de Unitate Ecclesiæ,* p 109 Edit.
Pearson

"sins, he is both sanctified and made a Temple of God, ‡ I ask of what God? If of the *Creator*, he could not be made his Temple, who believes not in *Him*; if of *Christ*; neither can he be made *His*, who denies *Christ* to be *God*: if of the *Holy Ghost*, *since the Three are One*, how can the *Holy Ghost* be reconciled to him, who is an enemy to either the *Father* or the *Son*?" But here it is to be noted, that Cyprian does not say in either of these places, "the Father, Word and Holy Ghost"; as the text now has it; but in the former passage, "the Father, Son and Holy Ghost", and in the latter, " the Creator, Christ and Holy Ghost"; and in neither place cites any thing more of the text than these words, " and these Three are One". The whole difficulty then rests here, how Cyprian came to say, " It is written of the *Father, Son and Holy*

" ‡ Quæro cujus Dei? Si *Creatoris*, non potuit, qui in eum non credit; Si *Christi*, nec hujus fieri potest templum, qui negat *Deum Christum*, Si *Spiritus Sancti, cum Tres Unum sint*, quomodo Spiritus Sanctus placatus esse ei potest, qui aut Patris aut Filii inimicus est?"—*Cyprian. Epist. ad Jubaianum*, p 203. *Edit. Pearson.*

"*Ghost*; and *these Three are One*": and of this I am now to give an Account.

It will then be found, that both the Latins and the Greeks did soon after generally interpret these words, " the Spirit, the Water " and the Blood", to denote, in their mistical sense, "the Father, Son and Holy Ghost". And if so; it will be no hard thing to suppose Cyprian to do the same. St. Austin *(contra Maximinum)* after challenging his antagonist to produce one instance, either in the Old or New Testament, where two or more things of different natures or substances are conjoined; that is, where it is said of them, UNUM SUNT, (they are one) to guard against an obvious objection, thus goes on. ‖ " I

" ‖ Sane falli te nolo in epistolâ Johannis apostoli, " ubi ait, *Tres sunt Testes, Spiritus, Aqua et Sanguis:* " *et Tres Unum sunt.* Propter hoc admonui, ne falla- " ris. Hæc enim sacramenta sunt, in quibus, non " quid sint, sed quid ostendant, semper attenditur; " quoniam signa sunt rerum, aliud existentiâ, et aliud " significantiâ. Si ergo illa, quæ his significantur, " intelliguntur, ipsa inveniuntur unius esse substantiæ.— " De quibus (nempe *Patre, Filio Sanctoque Spiritu*) " verissime dici potest, *Tres sunt Testes, et Tres Unum* " *sunt*; ut nomine *Spiritus* significatum accipiamus, " *Deum Patrem,*—Nomine autem *Sanguinis, Filium,*— " Et nomine *Aquæ, Spiritum Sanctum.*" —*Augustin. contra Maximin.* Lib. III. cap. 22.

" would

" would not have you be deceived by the
" Epiftle of St. JOHN, where he fays, *There
" are Three Witneſſes, the Spirit, the Water
" and the Blood: and the Three are One.*
" For theſe are miſterious words, in which
" we are always to mind, not what they
" uſually import, but what they ſtand for;
" for they are ſymbols of things and dif-
" ferent in ſignification from their nature.
" If then thoſe things, which are ſignified
' by theſe words, are rightly comprehended,
" theſe will be found to be of one ſubſtance.
" —Of which (namely, *the Father, Son and
" Holy Ghoſt*) it may be truly ſaid, *They are
" Three Witneſſes, and the Three are One*;
" ſo that by *The Spirit* we ſhould un-
" derſtand *God the Father*,— alſo by the
' word *Blood, The Son*;—and by the *Water,
" The Holy Ghoſt.*" Thus did St. Auſtin
manifeſtly interpret " the Spirit, Water
" and Blood', miſtically to denote, " the
" Father, Son and Holy Ghoſt"; and neither
in this, nor any other part of his writings,
does he make the leaſt mention of the
" three witneſſes in Heaven", any other than as
ſignified in the miſterious ſenſe of the words,
" Spirit, Water and Blood". And whenever
he names them, it is not ſo, as we find it
in

in our present books, "the Father, Word and "Holy Ghost". Nor indeed is it to be imagin'd that St. Austin, or any other Father, who gave such an interpretation, could have read in his books, the testimony of "the Three in "Heaven".—In like manner Eucherius, Bishop of Lyons, in his questions upon this very Epistle of St. JOHN, informs us, that " the " Spirit, Water and Blood", was generally interpreted in this mistical way, though in a manner somewhat different from St. Austin. His words are, § " *Quest.* John in his epistle " lays down; *There are Three things that* " *bear record, the Water, the Blood and* " *the Spirit*; What is meant by this? " *Answer.* Some expound differently, but " most persons understand it of the Trinity " itself by a mistical interpretation—— " by the *Water*, pointing out the *Father*; " by the *Blood*, shewing *Christ*; and by the

---

" § *Interrog.* In Epistola Johannes ponit, *Tria sunt*
" *quæ testimonium perhibent, Aqua, Sanguis et Spiritus.*
" *Quid in hoc indicatur?* *Resp.* Quidam ex hoc dis-
" putant, &c. plures tamen hic ipsam interpretatione
" mysticâ intelligunt Trinitatem.—*Aquâ* indicans
" *Patrem*, *Sanguine*, *Christum* demonstrans, *Spiritu*,
" *Sanctum Spiritum manifestans*"—*Eucherius Lugdunensis de Quæstionibus in Epistolam Johannis.*

" *Spi-*

"*Spirit*, manifesting the *Holy Ghost*."—— We may also determine, that the Bishop could not have in his copy the testimony of "the Three in Heaven"; as, I think, he must then have formed his question; upon the whole, not a part of the passage; and because he has omitted the words *in terrâ*, which is never done by those, who cite this testimony.

Moreover a passage in Facundus, an African Bishop, about the middle of the sixth century, will both confirm this interpretation of St. John, and make it probable, that Cyprian is to be so understood also. In his defence of the council of Chalcedon, addressed to the emperor Justinian, he quotes the passage thus: * " For St. John " the Apostle, in his epistle, says thus of the " Father, and Son, and Holy Ghost: *There " are Three that bear witness in Earth, the " Spirit, Water and Blood, and these Three*

" * Nam et Johannes Apostolus in epistolâ suâ de " Patre, et Filio, et Spiritu Sancto, sic dicit. *Tres sunt* " *qui testimonium dant in terrâ, Spiritus, Aqua et* " *Sanguis, et hi Tres Unum sunt.* In Spiritu significans " Patrem,—In *Aquâ* vero *Spiritum Sanctum* significans; ' —In *Sanguine* vero *Filium* significans."—*Facund.* " I pag. 16. Ex *Editione Sirmondi Parisiis*, 1629.

" are

" *are One*: by the *Spirit* denoting the *Fa-*
" *ther*; by the *Water*, signifying the *Holy*
" *Ghost*: and by the *Blood*, signifying the
" *Son*."—Thus Facundus, not only gives us
the mistic Interpretation of the " Spirit, Wa-
" ter and Blood"; but introduces it in the
very manner of Cyprian, and expresly tells
us, that he understood Cyprian to be of
the same opinion. Moreover Facundus can
hardly be thought to know any thing of the
testimony of " the Three in Heaven", since
he makes no use of it, when it would have
been far more to his purpose. The argument he was upon, was to prove the Unity of
" the Father, Son and Holy Ghost"; and here,
after the example of many before him, he
imploys the mistical interpretation of the
" Spirit, Water and Blood", for this purpose;
and because St. John says of them; " and
" these Three are One"; and this exposition,
supposing them Symbols of the Three Persons of the Trinity, he makes use of it †

in

---

† The EDITOR must inform the reader, that thus
far is not Sir ISAAC's; the Copy transmitted to him
fairly acknowledges it, and adds, that the four first
paragraphs of the Manuscript are lost; and that as there
were no hopes of recovering them, they were supplied,

not

in order to prove them *One God.* ‡

These passages in Cyprian may receive further light by a like passage in Tertullian, from whence Cyprian seems to have borrowed them. For it is well known, that Cyprian was a great admirer of Tertullian's writings, and read them frequently, calling Tertullian his master. The passage is this, ¶

---

not out of vanity, but merely to lay before the reader those passages, which the letter itself plainly shews had been made use of by the author himself, and to the purposes, as is apprehended, they are here subservient to; and an assurance is also given, that all which follows the words " He makes use of it" are Sir ISAAC's own without alteration.

" *Tres Unum* esse dicuntur, possunt Spiritus, aut Aquæ,
" aut Sanguines dici? Quod tamen Johannis Apostoli
" testimonium B. Cyprianus Carthaginensis Antistes
" et Martyr, in epistola, sive libro, quem de Trinitate
" (imo de Unitate ecclesiæ) scripsit, de Patre, Filio
" et Spiritu Sancto dictum intelligit. Ait enim, *Dicit*
" *Dñs, Ego et Pater Unum sumus,* et iterum de
" Patre, Filio, et Spiritu Sancto scriptum est, *et hi Tres*
" *Unum sunt.*—*Fulgentius, cap.* I. *pag.* 16. *ibidem.*

" Connexus Patris in Filio, et Filii in Paracleto
" tres efficit cohærentes, alterum ex altero, *Qui*
" *Tres Unum sint,* (non Unus) quomodo dictum est.
" *Ego et Pater Unum sumus,* ad substantiæ Unitatem,
" non ad numeri Singularitatem."—*Tertullian advers.*
Prax. c. 25.

" The

" The connection of the Father in the Son,
" and of the Son in the Paraclete, makes
" *Three* coherent ones from one another,
" *which Three are One,* (one thing, not one
" person) as it is said, *I and the Father are*
" *One,* denoting the Unity of substance, not
" the singularity of number". Here, you see, Tertullian says not; " the Father, Word
" and Holy Ghost", as the text now has it,
" but the Father, Son and Paraclete"; nor cites any thing more of the text, than these words; " which Three are One". These he interprets of the Trinity, and inforces the interpretation by that other text; " I and the
" Father are One"; as if the phrase was of the same importance in both places.

So then, this interpretation seems to have been invented by the Montanists for giving countenance to their Trinity. For Tertullian was a Montanist, when he wrote this; and it is most likely that so corrupt and forced an interpretation had its rise among a sect of men, accustomed to make bold with the scriptures. Cyprian being accustomed to it in his master's writings, it seems from thence to have dropt into *his,* as may be gathered by the likeness between their citations. And by the disciples of these two great men, it seems to have been propagated

gated among those many Latins, who (as Eucherius tells us) received it in the next age, understanding the Trinity by the " Spirit, " Water and Blood". For how, without the countenance of some such authority, an interpretation so corrupt and strained, should come to be received in that age so generally, I do not understand.

And what is said of the testimony of Cyprian, may be much more said of *that* in the feigned disputation of Athanasius with Arius at Nice. For there the words cited are only, " καὶ οἱ τρεῖς τὸ ἕν εἰσιν"; and " these Three " are One"; and they are taken out of the eighth verse, without naming the persons of the Trinity before them. For the Greeks interpreted " the Spirit, Water and Blood", of the Trinity, as well as the Latins; as is manifest from the annotations they made on this text in the margin of some of their manuscripts.

For Father Simon *(Critical History of the New Test. chap. 18)* informs us, that in one of the MSS in the Library of the King of France, marked Num. 2247, over against these words; " ὅτι τρεῖς εἰσιν οἱ μαρτυροῦντες ἐν τῇ " γῆ (suspicor, ἐν τῇ γῇ, non extare in MS) τὸ " πνεῦμα καὶ τὸ ὕδωρ καὶ τὸ αἷμα". " For there
" are

(17)

" are Three that bear record in earth, the
" Spirit, the Water and the Blood"; there is
this remark, " τετέςι τὸ πνεῦμα τὸ ἅγιον καὶ ὁ
" πατὴρ καὶ αὐτὸς ἑαυτῦ"; that is, " the Holy
" Ghoſt, and the Father, and He of Himſelf".
—And in the ſame Copy over againſt theſe
words, " καὶ οἱ τρεῖς εἰς τὸ ἕν εἰσι", " and theſe
" Three are One"; this note is added, " τε-
" τέςι μία θεότης εἷς θεός". That is, "One Deity,
" One God". This MS is about 500 years old.

Alſo in the margin of one of the MSS
in Monſieur Colbert's Library, Num 871.
Father Simon tells us, there is a like remark.
For, beſides theſe words, " εἷς θεὸς μία θεότης",
" One God, One Godhead", there are added,
" μαρτυρία τῦ θεῦ τῦ πατρὸς καὶ τῦ ἁγίε
" πνεύματος". " The Teſtimony of God
" the Father, and of the Holy Ghoſt".

Theſe marginal notes ſufficiently ſhew
how the Greeks uſed to apply this text to
the Trinity, and by conſequence, how the
author of that diſputation is to be underſtood.
But I ſhould tell you alſo, that that diſputation was not wrote by Athanaſius, but by a
later author, and therefore as a ſpurious piece
uſes not to be much inſiſted on.

Now this miſtical application of " the
" Spirit, Water and Blood", to ſignify the
C   Trinity,

Trinity, seems to me to have given occasion to some body, either fraudulently to insert the testimony of " the Three in Heaven", in express words into the text, for proving the Trinity, or else to note it in the margin of his book, by way of interpretation. Whence it might afterwards creep into the text in transcribing

And the first upon record, that inserted it, is Jerome, if the preface [*] to the

---

[*] The whole preface runs thus " Incipit prologus in epistolas canonicas. *Non ita est ordo apud Græcos, qui integrè sapiunt, fidemque rectam sectantur, epistolarum septem, quæ canonicæ nuncupantur, sicut in Latinis codicibus invenitur. Ut qua Petrus est primus in ordine Apostolorum, primæ sint etiam ejus epistolæ in ordine cæterarum. Sed sicut Evangelistas dudum ad veritatis lineam correximus, ita has proprio ordini, Deo juvante, reddidimus. Est enim una earum prima Jacobi, duæ Petri, tres Johannis, et Judæ una. Quæ si sic ut ab eis digestæ sunt, ita quoque ab interpretibus fideliter in Latinum verterentur eloquium, nec ambiguitatem legentibus facerent, nec sermonum sese varietates impugnarent, illo præcipuè loco ubi de Unitate Trinitatis in prima Johannis epistola, positam legimus. In quâ etiam ab infidelibus translatoribus, multum erratum esse a fidei veritate comperimus, trium tantummodo vocabula, hoc est, Aquæ, Sanguinis et Spiritus, in ipsa sua editione ponentibus, et Patris, Verbique, ac Spiritus testimonium omittentibus: in quo maximè et fides Catholica roboratur, et Patris, ac Filii, et Spiritus una divinitatis substantia comprobatur. In cæteris verò epistolis.*

canonical epistles, which goes under his name, be His. For whilst he composed not a new translation of the New Testament, but only corrected the ancient vulgar Latin (as learned men think) and among his Emendations (written perhaps at first in the margin of his book) he inserted this testimony, he complains in the said preface, how he was thereupon accused by some of the Latins, for falsifying Scripture, and makes answer, that former Latin translators had much erred from the faith, in putting only, " the Spirit, Water and Blood" in their edition, and omitting the testimony of " the " Three in Heaven", whereby the Catholic Faith is established. In this defence he seems to say, that he corrected the vulgar Latin translation by the original Greek; and this is the great testimony the text relies upon.

---

epistolis, quantum à nostrâ, aliorum distet editio, lectoris judicio derelinquo. Sed tu, virgo Christi Eustochium, dum à me impensius scripturæ veritatem inquiris, meam quodammodo senectutem invidorum dentibus corrodendam exponis, qui me falsarium, corruptoremque Sanctarum pronunciant Scripturarum. Sed ego in tali opere, nec æmulorum meorum invidiam pertimesco, nec Sanctæ Scripturæ veritatem poscentibus denegabo".

But whilst he confesses it was not in the Latin before, and accuses former translators of falsifying the scriptures in omitting it, he satisfies us, that it has crept into the Latin since his time, and so cuts off all the authority of the present vulgar Latin for justifying it. And whilst he was accused by his cotemporaries of falsifying the Scriptures in inserting it, this accusation also confirms, that he altered the publick reading. For had the reading been dubious before he made it so, no man would have charged him with falsification for following either part.

Also, whilst upon this accusation he recommends the alteration by its usefulness for establishing the Catholick Faith, this renders it the more suspected by discovering both the design of his making it, and the ground of his hoping for success. However, seeing he was thus accused by his cotemporaries, it gives us just reason to examine the business between him and his accusers. And so, he being called to the bar, we are not to lay stress upon his own testimony for himself (for no man is a witness in his own cause) but laying aside all prejudice, we ought, according to the ordinary rules of justice, to examine the business

ness between him and his accusers by other witnesses.

They, that have been conversant in his writings, observe a strange liberty, which he takes in asserting things. Many notable instances of this he has left us in composing those very fabulous lives of Paul and Hilarian, not to mention what he has written upon other occasions. Whence Erasmus said of him, that he was in affirming things, † "frequently violent and impudent, and often " contrary to himself". But I accuse him not. It is possible, that he might be sometimes imposed upon, or, through inadvertency, commit a mistake. Yet since his cotemporaries accused him, it is but just, that we should lay aside the prejudice of his great name, and hear the cause impartially between them.

Now the witnesses between them are partly the ancient translators of the scriptures into the various languages, partly the writers of his own age, and of the ages

---

" † Sæpe numero violentus, parumque pudens, sæpe " varius, parumque sibi constans "
Erasmi Annotation. in Johan v. 7.
Vide etiam, quæ Erasmus contra Leum in hunc locum de Hieronimo fusius dixit.

next before, and after him, and partly the scribes who have copied out the Greek manuscripts of the scriptures in all ages. And all these are against him. For by the unanimous evidence of all these, it will appear that the testimony of " the Three in " Heaven" was wanting in the Greek manuscripts, from whence Jerome, or whoever was the author of that preface to the canonical epistles, pretends to have borrowed it.

The ancient interpreters, which I cite, as witnesses against him, are chiefly the authors of the ancient *vulgar Latin*, of the *Syriac* and the *Æthiopic* versions. For as he tells us, that the Latins omitted the testimony of " the Three in Heaven" in their version before his time, so in the Syriac and Æthiopic versions (both which, from Bishop Walton's account of them, are much ancienter than Jerome's time, being the versions which the Oriental and Æthiopic nations received from the beginning, and generally used, as the Latins did the vulgar Latin) that same testimony is wanting to this day, and the authors of these *Three* most ancient, most famous, and most received versions by omitting it are concurrent witnesses,

witnesses, that they found it wanting in the original Greek manuscripts of their own times.

It is wanting also in other ancient versions, as in the *Ægyptian Arabick*, published in Walton's Polyglot Bible, in the *Armenian* version, ‡ used, ever since Chrysostom's age, by the Armenian Nations, and in the Illyrican ¶ of Cyrillus, used in Rascia, Bulgaria, Moldavia, Russia, Muscovy, and other countries, which use the Sclavonic Tongue. In a copy of this version, ¶ printed at Ostrobe (Ostrow) in Volhinia, in the Year 1581, I have seen it wanting, and one Camillus § relates the same thing out

---

‡ " Codex Armeniacus ante 400 annos exaratus, " quem vidi apud Episcopum Ecclesiæ Armeniacæ, quæ " Amstellodami colligitur, locum illum non legit"— *Sandius Append Interpret Paradox in h l.*

¶ The printed Sclavonic version runs thus " *Quia* " *Tres sunt, qui testificantur, Spiritus, et Aqua, et San-* " *guis, et Tres in Unum sunt. Si testimonium, &c* "

" § Testimonium *trium in Cœlo* non est in antiquissi- " mis Illyricorum et Ruthenorum codicibus, quorum " unum exemplar à sexcentis ferè annis manuscriptum, " jampridem apud illustrissimum Gabrielem Chineum, " terræ Bactricæ Dominum vidi, et legi alterum " manibus nostris teritur, fide et antiquitate suâ nobile.— *Camillus de Antichristo.* Lib II cap. 2 Pag 156

of ancient Manuscripts of this version seen by him.

Nor do I know of any version, wherein it is extant, except the *modern vulgar Latin*, and such *modern versions* of the Western Nations, as have been influenced by it. So then, by the unanimous consent of all the ancient and faithful interpreters, which we have hitherto met with (who doubtless made use of the best Manuscripts they could get) the Testimony of " the Three in Heaven" was not anciently in the Greek.

And that it was neither in the ancient versions, nor in the Greek; but was wholly unknown to the first Churches, is most certain by an argument hinted above, namely, that in all that vehement, universal, and lasting Controversy about the Trinity in Jerome's time, and both before, and long enough after it, this text of " the Three in " Heaven" was never once thought of. It is now in every body's mouth, and accounted the main Text for the business, and would assuredly have been so too with them, had it been in their books. And yet it is not once to be met with in all the disputes, epistles, orations, and other writings of the Greeks and Latins (Alexander of Alexandria,

dria, Athanasius, the council of Sardica, Basil, Nazienzen, Nyssen, Epiphanius, Chrysostom, Cyril, Theodoret, Hilary, Ambrose, Austin, Victorinus Afer, Philastrius Brixiensis, Phæbedius Agennensis, Gregorius Bæticus, Faustinus Diaconus, Paschasius, Arnobius Junior, Cerealis, and others) in the times of those controversies; no, not in Jerome himself; if his version and preface to the Canonical Epistles be excepted.

The writings of those times were very many, and copious; and there is no argument, or Text of Scripture, which they do not urge again and again. That of St. John's Gospel, " I, and the Father, am " One", is every where inculcated, but this of " the Three in Heaven, and their " being One", is no where to be met with, 'till at length, when the ignorant ages came on, it began by degrees to creep into the Latin copies out of Jerome's version.

So far are they from citing the testimony of " the Three in Heaven", that, on the contrary, as often as they have occasion to mention the place, they omit it, and that too, as well after Jerome's age, as in, and before

fore it. For Hesychius (in *Levit.* Lib. ii. cap 8. *post med.*) cites the place thus. " Audi Johannem dicentem, Tria sunt, " qui testimonium præbent, et Tres Unum " sunt, Spiritus, et Sanguis et Aqua". The words, *in terrâ*, he omits, which is never done, but in Copies, where " the Three " in Heaven" is wanting. Cassiodorus, or whoever was the Author of the Latin version of the Discourse of Clemens Alexandrinus on these Epistles of St. John reads it thus. ' Quia Tres sunt, qui testificantur, " Spiritus, et Aqua, et Sanguis, et hi Tres " Unum sunt". (N. B. It is called so in *Biblioth. S. patrum*, Edit. Paris. 1589)

Bede in his Commentary on the place reads it thus. " Et Spiritus est, qui testi- " ficatur, quoniam Christus est veritas. Quo- " niam Tres sunt, qui testimonium dant in " terrâ, Spiritus, Aqua, et Sanguis, et Tres " Unum sunt. Si testimonium, &c." But here the words, *in terrâ*, so far as I can gather from his Commentary on this text have been inserted by some later Hand. —The Author of the first Epistle, ascribed to Pope Eusebius, reads it, as Bede does, omitting only the words, *in terrâ*.——And if

if the Authority of Popes be valuable, Pope Leo, the Great, in his tenth Epistle, thus cites the place. "Et Spiritus est, qui
"testificatur, quoniam Spiritus est veritas;
"quia Tres sunt, qui testimonium dant, Spi-
"ritus, et Aqua, et Sanguis, et hi Tres
"Unum sunt".

St. Ambrose, in the sixth chapter of his first Book, *de Spiritu Sancto*, disputing for the Unity of the Three Persons, says, "Hi Tres Unum sunt, *Johannes dixit*,
"Aqua, Sanguis et Spiritus: Unum in
"misterio; non in natura". This is all he could find of the text, while he was disputing about the Trinity, and therefore he proves the Unity of the Persons by the mistical Unity of the Spirit, Water and Blood, interpreting these of the Trinity with Cyprian and others. Yea, in the eleventh chapter of his third book, he fully recites the text thus. "Per Aquam
"et Sanguinem venit Christus Jesus, non
"solum in Aquâ, sed in Aquâ et Sanguine;
"et Spiritus testimonium dat, quoniam Spi-
"ritus est veritas. Quia Tres sunt Testes,
"Spiritus, Aqua, et Sanguis; et hi Tres
"Unum sunt in Christo Jesu". See also Ambrose

Ambrose in Luc. xxii. 10. and in his book, *De iis qui mysteriis initiantur*, cap. IV.

The like reading of Facundus, Eucherius, and St. Austin you have in the places cited above. These are Latins, as late, or later, than Jerome. For Jerome did not prevail with the Churches of his own time to receive the testimony of " the Three in " Heaven". And for them to know his version, and not receive his testimony was in effect to condemn it.

And as for the Greeks, Cyril of Alexandria reads the text without this testimony in the xivth book of his Thesaurus, cap. 5, and again in his first book *de fide ad Reginas*, a little after the middle. And so does Oecumenius, a later Greek, in his Commentary on this place of St. John's Epistle. Also Didimus Alexandrinus, in his Commentary on the same passage, reads " the " Spirit, Water and Blood", without mentioning, " the Three in Heaven"; and so he does in his book of the Holy Ghost, where he seems to omit nothing, that he could find for his purpose; and so does Gregory Nazienzen in his xxxvith Oration concerning the Holy Ghost; and also, Nicetus

cetus in his Commentary on Gregory Nazienzen's xlivth Oration.

And here it is farther obfervable, that, as the Eufebians had contended, that " the " Father, Son and Holy Ghoſt" were not to be connumerated, becauſe they were things of a different kind, Nazienzen and Nicetus anſwer, that they might be connumerated, becauſe St. John connumerates three things not confubſtantial, namely, " the Spirit, the " Water, and the Blood ". By the objection of the Eufebians, it then appears, that the Teſtimony of " the Three in Heaven" was not in their books, and by the anſwer of the Catholicks it is as evident, that it was not in *theirs*. For while they anſwer by inſtancing in " the Spirit, Water and Blood ", they could not have miſſed of, " the Father, the " Word, and the Holy Ghoſt "; had they been connumerated, and called one in the words immediately before; and to anſwer, by inſtancing in *theſe*, would have been far more to their purpoſe, becauſe it was the very thing in queſtion.

In like manner the Eunomians, in diſputing againſt the Catholicks, had objected, that the Holy Ghoſt is no where in Scripture

conjoined

conjoined with the Father and the Son, except in the form of Baptism: which is as much as to say, that the Testimony of "the Three in Heaven" was not in their books: and yet St Basil (lib. v. *adversus Eunomium sub finem*) whilst he is very diligent in returning an answer to them, and perplexes himself in citing places, which are nothing to the purpose, does not produce this text of "the Three in Heaven", though it be the most obvious, and the only proper passage, had it been then in the Scriptures, and therefore, he knew nothing of it. The objection of the Eunomians, and the answer of the Catholicks, sufficiently shew, that it was in the books of neither party.

Besides all this, the tenth Epistle of Pope Leo, mentioned above, was that very famous Epistle to Flavian, Patriarch of Constantinople against Eutiches, which went about through all the Churches both Eastern and Western, being translated into Greek, and sent about in the East by Flavian. It was generally applauded in the West, and read in the council of Chalcedon, and there solemnly approved and subscribed by all the Bishops, and in this Epistle the text was
thus

thus cited. " Et Spiritus est, qui testifica-
" tur, quoniam Christus est veritas: quia
" Tres sunt, qui testimonium dant, Spiritus,
" Aqua, et Sanguis; et hi Tres Unum sunt".
And by putting πνεῦμά (according to the Greek reading) for *Christus*, which is still the vulgar Latin, it was thus translated.
" καὶ τὸ πνεῦμά ἐςιν τὸ μαρ]υροῦν· ἐπειδὴ τὸ
" πνεῦμά ἐςιν ἡ ἀλήθεια· τρεῖς γὰρ εἰσιν οἱ μαρ-
"]υροῦν]ες τὸ πνεῦμά, καὶ τὸ ὕδωρ, καὶ τὸ αἷμα·
" καὶ οἱ τρεῖς τὸ ἓν εἰσι."

So then we have the reading quoted by the Pope, owned in the West, and solemnly subscribed in the East by the fourth general council, and therefore it continued, the publick received reading in both the East and West, till after the age of that council.

So then the testimony of " the Three " in Heaven", which, in the times of these controversies, would have been in every body's mouth, had it been in their books, was wholly unknown to the Churches of those ages. All that they could find in their books was the testimony of " the " Water, the Spirit and the Blood".

Will you now say, that the testimony of " the Three in Heaven", was razed out of their

their books by the prevailing Arrians? Yes truly, those Arrians were crafty knaves, that could conspire so cunningly and slily all the world over at once (as at the command of a Mithridates) in the latter end of the reign of Constantius to get all men's books in their hands, and correct them without being perceived: ay, and conjurers too, without leaving any blot or chasm in their books, whereby the knavery might be suspected and discovered; and to wipe away the memory of it out of all men's brains; so that neither Athanasius, nor any body else, could afterwards remember, that they had ever seen it in their books before; and out of their own books too, so that, when they turned to the Consubstantial Faith, as they generally did in the West, soon after the Death of Constantius, they could then remember no more of it, than any body else.

Well then, it was out of their books in Jerome's age, when he pretended it was in; which is the point we are to prove, and when any body can shew, that it was in their books before, it may be pertinent to consider that point also: but till then we are only to enquire how, since it was out, it came into

the

the copies, that are now extant. For they, that without proof accuse the Hereticks of corrupting books, and upon that pretence correct them at their pleasure without the Authority of ancient Manuscripts (as some learned men in the fourth and fifth centuries used to do) are Falsaries by their own confession, and certainly need no other confutation. And therefore, if this reading was once out, we are bound in justice to believe, that it was out from the beginning; unless the razing of it out can be proved by some better argument, than that of pretence and clamour.

Will you now say, that Jerome followed some copy different from any, which the Greeks were acquainted with? This is to overthrow the authority of his version by making him depart from the received Greek, and besides, it is contrary to what he himself seems to represent. For in his blaming not the vulgar Greek copies, but the Latin interpreters only, which were before his time, as if they had varied from the received Greek, he represents, that he himself followed it. He does not excuse, and justify himself for reading differently from the received Greek, in order to follow a private copy, but accuses former Interpreters, as if, in leaving out the testimony of "the Three in Heaven", they had not followed the received Greek.

And therefore, since the Greeks knew nothing of this Testimony, the authority of his version sinks; and that the rather, because he was then accused of corrupting the Text, and could not persuade either the Greeks or the Latins of those times to receive his reading. For the Latins received it not, till many years after his death; and the Greeks not till this present age, when the Venetians sent it amongst them in printed books: And their not receiving it was plainly to approve the accusation.

The authority of this version being thus far discussed, it remains, that we consider the authority of the Manuscripts, wherein we now read the testimony of "the Three in "Heaven". And by the best inquiry, that I have been able to make, it is wanting in the Manuscripts of all Languages, but the Latin. For, as we have shewn, that the Æthiopick, Syriac, Arabick, Armenian and Sclavonian versions, still in use in the several Eastern nations, Ethiopia, Egypt, Syria,
Meso-

Mesopotamia, Armenia, Muscovy, and some others, are strangers to this reading: so I am told by those, who have been in Turkey, that it is wanting to this day in the Greek Manuscripts, which have been brought from thence into the West, and that the Greeks, now that they have got it in print from the Venetians, when their Manuscripts are objected against it, pretend, that the Arians erazed it.

A reading then, to be found in no manuscripts, but the Latin ones, and not in the Latin before Jerome's age, as Jerome himself confesses, can be but of little authority, and we have already proved it to be spurious by shewing, that it was heretofore unknown both to the Western, and the Eastern Churches in the times of the great controversy about the Trinity.

But, however, for your further satisfaction, we shall now give you an account of these Manuscripts, shewing, first, *how*, in the dark ages, it crept into the Latin Manuscripts, out of Jerome's version; and then, *how* it lately crept out of the Latin into the printed Greek, those, who first published it in Greek, having never yet so much as seen it in any Greek Manuscript.

That the vulgar Latin, now in use, is a mixture of the old vulgar Latin, and of Jerome's version together, is the received opinion. Few of these Manuscripts are above four or five hundred years old. The latest generally have the testimony of " the Three " in Heaven": the oldest of all usually want it, which shews that it has crept in by degrees. Erasmus notes it to be wanting in three very ancient ones; one of which was in the Pope's library at Rome, the other two were at Bruges; and he adds, that in another Manuscript, belonging to the library of the Minorites in Antwerp, the testimony of " the Three in Heaven", was noted in the margin in a newer hand.

Peter Cholinus notes in the margin of his Latin edition of the Scriptures, printed Anno Christi, 1543, and 1544, that it was wanting in the most ancient Manuscript of the Tugurine library. Dr. Burnet has lately noted it to be wanting in some other ancient ones. An ancient and diligent collater of Manuscripts, cited by Lucas Brugensis by the name of Epanorthotes notes in general, that

it

it was wanting in the ancient Latin Manuscripts. Lucas Brugensis himself, collating many Latin ones, notes it to be wanting in only FIVE, that is, in the few old ones, which he had, his Manuscripts being almost all of them new ones. For he *(calce annotat.)* praises the Codex Lobiensis written Anno Christi, 1084, and the Codex Tornacensis written Anno Christi, 1105, as most ancient and venerable for antiquity, and used others much more new, of which a great number was easily had, such as was the Codex Buslidianus, written Anno Christi, 1432, that is, but eight years before the invention of printing.

The Lateran council, collected under Innocent the Third, Anno Christi, 1215, Canon 2. mentions Joachim, the abbot, quoting the text in these words. " Quoniam in ca-
" nonicâ Johannis epistolâ legitur, *quia Tres*
" *sunt, qui testimonium dant in Cælo, Pater,*
" *et Verbum, et Spiritus; et hi Tres Unum*
" *sunt:* statimque subjungitur. *Et Tres sunt,*
" *qui testimonium dant in terrâ, Spiritus, Aqua,*
" *et Sanguis, et Tres Unum sunt · sicut in*
" *codicibus quibusdam invenitur*".---This was

written

written by Joachim * in the papacy of Alexander the Third, that is, in or before the year 1180, and therefore this reading was then got but into some books. For the words, " Sicut in codicibus quibusdam invenitur", refer as well to the first words of Joachim, " Quoniam in canonicâ Joannis epistolâ legi-
" tur" as to the next, " statimque subjungi-
" tur"; and more to the first, than the next; because the first part of the citation was then, but in some books, as appears by ancient Manuscripts; but the second part was in almost all: the words, " Tres Unum sunt", being in all the books which wanted the testimony of " the Three in Heaven"; and in most of those, which had it; though afterwards left out in many, when branded by the schoolmen for Arian.

But to go to the bottom of the corruption. Gregory the Great † writes, that Jerome's version was in use in his time, and therefore, no wonder, if the testimony of " the Three " in Heaven" began to be cited out of it before. Eugenius, bishop of Carthage, in the

---

* Vid Math Paris Histor Angl A D 1179.

† Vid. Walton Prolegomena x. 55.

seventh year of Hunneric, king of the Vandals, Anno Christi 484, in the summary of his faith exhibited to the king, cited it the first of any man, so far as I can find. A while after Fulgentius, another African bishop, disputing against the same Vandals, cited it again, and backed it with the forementioned place of Cyprian, applied to the testimony of "the Three in Heaven".------And so it is probable, that by that abused authority of Cyprian it began first in Africk, in the disputes with the ignorant Vandals, to get some credit; and thence at length crept into use. It occurs also frequently in Vigilius Tapsensis, another African bishop, cotemporary to Fulgentius.

In its defence some alledge earlier writers; namely, the first epistle of pope Hyginus, the first epistle of pope John II. the book of Idacius Clarus against Varimadus; and the book, *De unitâ Deitate Trinitatis*, ascribed to Athanasius. But Chiffletius, who published the works of Victor Vitensis, and Vigilius Tapsensis, sufficiently proves the book against Varimadus to be this Vigilius's, and erroneously ascribed to Idacius.------To the same Vigilius he asserts also the book,

De unitá Deitate Trinitatis. Certainly Athanasius was not its author.———All the epistles of Hyginus, except the beginning, and the end; and the first part of the epistle of pope John, wherein the testimony of " the Three " in Heaven" is cited, are nothing else than fragments of the book against Varimadus, described word for word by some forger of decretal epistles, as may appear by comparing them; so then Eugenius is the first upon record, that quotes it.

But though he set it on foot among the Africans; yet I cannot find, that it became of authority in Europe, before the revival of learning, in the twelfth and thirteenth Centuries. In those ages, Saint Barnard, the Schoolmen, Joachim, and the Lateran council spread it abroad, and scribes began generally to insert it into the text: but in such Latin Manuscripts and European writers, as are ancienter than those times, it is scarce to be met with.

Now that it was inserted into the vulgar Latin out of Jerome's version is manifest by the manner, how the vulgar Latin, and that version came to be mixed. For it is agreed, that the Latins, after Jerome's version began to be of ufe, noted out of it his corrections of the vulgar Latin in the margin of their books. And thefe the tranfcribers afterwards inferted into the text. By this means, the old Latin has been fo generally corrected, that it is no where to be found fince. It is Jerome's, that we now read, and not the old vulgar Latin; and what wonder, if in Jerome we read the teftimony of "the Three in Heaven"? For who, that inferted the reft of Jerome's corrections into the text, would leave out fuch a paffage for the Trinity, as this hath been taken to be?

But to put the queftion out of difpute, there are footfteps of the infertion ftill remaining. For in fome old Manufcripts, it has been found noted in the margin; in others to be various readings, and when it is found inferted into the text, it is plainly fuch as ought to arife by tranfcribing it out of the margin into the text. I fhall only mention the three following varieties.

Of the Manufcripts, which have not the teftimony of " the Three in Heaven". Some have the words *in terrâ*, in the eighth verfe, but the moft want it; which feems to proceed from hence, that fome, before they

allowed

allowed so great an addition to the text, as the testimony of " the Three in Heaven" noted only *in terrâ*, in the margin of their books.

Of the Manuscripts, which have the testimony of " the Three in Heaven", some in the eighth verse have " Hi Tres Unum sunt". Others not. The reason of this seems to be, that of those, who noted this testimony in the margin, some blotted out, " Et hi " Tres Unum sunt" in the eighth verse, according to Jerome, and others did not.

And lastly, the testimony of " the Three " in Heaven" is in most books set before the testimony of " the Three in Earth"; in some, it is set after. So Erasmus notes two old books, in which it is set after; Lucas Brugensis a third; and Hesselius (if I misremember not) a fourth; and so Vigilius Tapsensis * sets it after: which seems to proceed from hence, that it was sometimes so noted in the margin, that the reader, or transcriber knew not, whether it were to come before, or after. Now these discords in the Latin Manuscripts, as they detract from the

---

* Vigilius hor. adverf. Varimadum. cap. 5.

authority of the Manuscripts; so they confirm to us, that the old vulgar Latin has in these things been tampered with, and corrected by Jerome's version.

In the next place, I am to shew *how*, and *when*, the testimony of " the Three in Hea-" ven" crept out of the Latin into the Greek. —Those, who printed the Greek Testament, did generally in following their Manuscripts omit the testimony of " the Three in Hea-" ven", except in *Spain*. For it was omitted in the first and second edition of Erasmus, Anno Christi, 1516 and 1519.—In the edition of Francis Asulan, printed at Venice by Aldus, Anno Christi, 1518;—In that of Nicholas Gerbelius, printed at Haganau, Anno Christi, 1521;——And a little after, in that of Wolfius Cephalius, printed at Strasbourg, Anno Christi, 1524; and again in 1526, in the Badian edition, as Erasmus notes; and in that of Simon Colinæus at Paris, Anno Christi, 1534 *.——At the same time it was

---

* " In editis exemplaribus nonnullis non legi ut in " Aldinâ et Badianâ editione ——Addo, nec in Græco " Testamento Gerbelii Haganoæ, 1521, nec in Co-" linæi, Parisiis editione" *Vide etiam Gomarum in h. locum.*

omitted

omitted in some editions of the other Western languages, as in the Saxon and German editions of Luther, and in the Latin Tugurine editions of Peter Cholins, Anno Christi, 1543 and 1544.

The first edition in Greek, which has the testimony of "the Three in Heaven" was that of cardinal Ximenes, printed at Complutum in Spain, in 1515; but not published before the year 1521. The cardinal in his edition used the assistance of several divines, which he called together to Complutum, there founding an university, Anno Christi, 1517, or a little before. Two of these divines were Antonius Nebisensis and Stunica. For Stunica then resided at Complutum; and in the preface * to a treatise,

---

* "Cum præsertim, si quisquam alius, et nos quo-
"que his de rebus, nostro quodam jure, judicium ferre
"possimus Quippe qui non paucos annos in sanctis
"Scripturis veteris et Novi Testamenti, Hebraice, Græce,
"et Latine per legendis consumpserimus; ac Hebraica,
"Græcaque ipsa divinarum literarum exemplaria
"cum antiquissimis Latinorum, codicibus diligentissime
"contulerimus Longa igitur lectione, ac experientiâ
"tamdem edocti, quantum tralationi huic ecclesiastice
"Novi Testamenti deferendum sit, nisi fallor, optime
".... ——Hæc Stunica in prologo libri sui.

which

which he wrote against Erasmus, gives this testimony of himself; "That he had spent "some years in reading the Holy Scriptures "in Hebrew, Greek and Latin; and had "diligently collated the Hebrew and Greek "exemplars with the Latin copies". This book, displeasing the cardinal, was not printed till after his death, and then it came forth at Complutum, Anno Christi, 1520.——The year before, one Lee, an Englishman, writ also against Erasmus, and both *Stunica* and *Lee*, amongst other things, reprehended him for omitting the testimony of "the Three "in Heaven".

Afterwards Erasmus, finding the Spaniards, and some others of the Romish church in a heat against him, printed this testimony in his third edition, Anno Christi, 1522; representing, "That in his former editions he "had printed the text, as he found it in his "Manuscripts; but now there being found "in England one Manuscript, which had "the testimony of *the Three in Heaven*, he "had inserted it, according to that Manu- "script; for avoiding the calumnies raised "against him".——And so it continued in his two following editions.

And

(46)

And, at length, Robert Stephens, Anno Christi, 1550; reprinted Erasmus's edition, with some few alterations, and various lections, taken out of the Complutensian edition, and fifteen Greek Manuscripts, which he named after the numeral Greek Letters, α, ϛ, γ, δ, ε, &c. putting α for the Complutensian edition, and ϛ, γ, δ, ε, &c. for the Manuscripts in their order; and noting in the margin, that the testimony of "the Three in Heaven" was wanting in the seven Manuscripts, δ, ε, ζ, θ, ι, ια, ιγ.—— When Beza † tells us, that he had read it in the rest. His words are, " Legit Hie-
" ronimus, legit Erasmus in Britannico
" codice, et in Complutensi editione. Le-
" gimus et in nonnullis Roberti nostri vete-
" ribus libris'.

And this is the original and authority of the printed editions. For these are the editions ever since followed by all the West; and of late years propagated by the Venetian presses into Greece, and nothing further, that I know of, has been discovered in any Manuscripts in favour of these editions.

---

† Beza in hunc locum.

Now

Now to pull off the vizard, I cannot but, in the firſt place, extreamly complain of Beza's want of modeſty and caution in expreſſing himſelf. * In the preface to his annotations, deſcribing what helps he had in compoſing his firſt edition, he tells us, " That he had the annotations of Valla, " Stapulenſis and Eraſmus, and the writings " of the ancients and moderns collated by " himſelf; and out of Stephens's library " the exemplar, which Stephens had colla- " ted, with about twenty-five Manuſcripts, " almoſt all of which were printed". He ſhould have ſaid ſeventeen; for that number he puts in other places, and in his annotations cites no more. So then, he had the collations of two more Manuſcripts, than Stephens has given us in print. And this was all his furniture.

---

* " Non deſunt tamen, qui Bezam nimis audacem " fuiſſe judicant, dum à receptâ lectione ſæpius ſine " neceſſitate recedit, et unius, interdum nullius codicis " authoritate fretus, Prætoriam exercet poteſtatem ex " conjecturis mutando, et interpolando textum ſacrum " pro libitu".——*Walton Prolegomen.* IV. Sect. 15. *in Bibl. Polyglott.*

The

The original Manuscripts he does not here pretend to have, nor could he have them. For they were not Stephens's Manuscripts, but belonged to several libraries in France and Italy. The Manuscript, ϛ, Stephens himself never saw, but had only various lections collated out of it by his Friends in Italy. The Manuscripts γ, δ, ε, ϛ, ζ, η, ι, κ, were not Stephens's; but belonged to the library of the king of France, to whom Stephens was printer. The other six books, ί, ιβ, ιε, ιγ, ιδ, ιϛ, he had not out of his own library, but borrowed them for a time from several places to collate, his friends studying to promote the design of his edition.

And yet Beza, in his annotations, when he would favour any text, cites the collations of Stephens in such a manner, as if he had the very original Manuscripts at Geneva before his eyes. And, where Stephens does not cite various lections there, he reckons, that in the text of Stephens's collated book, he read all the Manuscripts. ——So in Mark, vi. 11. where Stephens notes a certain period to be wanting in the Manuscript copies, ϛ and ι, Beza saith,

" Hæc

" Hæc periodus in omnibus exemplaribus
" Græcis legitur, exceptis fecundo et octavo".
—— In the Acts xiii. 33. becaufe Stephens had noted no various lections, Beza affirms of the Greek text; " Ita fcriptum invenimus " in omnibus vetuftis codicibus". —— In 1 John iv. 3. where Stephens is filent, Beza fpeaks, " Sic legitur in omnibus Græcis ex- " emplaribus, quæ quidem mihi infpicere " licuit".—In James i. 22. where Stephens is again filent, Beza tells us of the word μόνον. " Ego in omnibus noftris vetuftis libris " inveni".——And fo, where Stephens in the margin had noted the teftimony of " the " Three in Heaven" to be wanting in feven Manufcripts, he thinks, that, in reading the text of Stephens's collated book, he reads it in the reft; and fo tells us, " Legimus et " nos in nonnullis Roberti Stephani codici- " bus". —— Thus he did in the firft edition of his annotations.

Afterwards, when he had got two real Manufcripts, the Claromontan, and that, which at length he prefented to the univer- fity of Cambridge; (in both which the ca- nonical epiftles are wanting) in the epiftle to his fourth edition, in reckoning up the books, he then used, he puts only these two, and the seventeen of Stephens; and, in his fifth edition, he writes summarily, that he used nineteen Manuscripts, joining with those two *real* ones, the collations of Stephens, as if in those he had seventeen others; which sufficiently explains his way of speaking in his annotations. But whilst he had not the Manuscripts themselves to read with his own eyes, it was too hard and unwarrantable a way of speaking to tell us. " Legimus et " nos in nonnullis Roberti Stephani codici- " bus"; and therefore, in his late editions, he corrects himself, and tells us only, that the reading doth " Extare in nonnullis Ste- " phani veteribus libris".

Thus Beza argues from Stephens's book of collations, and the same inference has been made by Lucas Brugensis, and others, ever since from Stephens's forementioned edition of his book. For, they say, " Ste- ' phens had fifteen Manuscripts in all, and " found the testimony of *the Three in Heaven* " wanting, but in seven; and therefore, it " was in the other eight; and so being " found in the greater part of his Manu- " scripts, has the authority of manuscripts
" on

" on its side.——Thus they argue; and this is the great argument, by which the printed Greek has hitherto been justified.

But if they plainly consider the business a little better, they will find themselves very much mistaken. For though Stephens had *fifteen* Manuscripts in all; yet all of them did not contain all the Greek Testament. *Four* of them, noted γ, ϛ, ιϛ, ιδ, had each of them the four gospels only.—— *Two*, noted ϛ, η, contained only the gospels, and the Acts of the Apostles.——*One*, noted ιϛ, contained the Apocalypse only.——*One*, noted ιε, had only the Apocalypse, with St. Paul's Epistles to the Corinthians, Galatians, Ephesians, Philippians and Colossians. —— The other *seven*, noted δ, ε, ζ, θ, ι, ια, ιγ, contained both St. Paul's Epistles, and the canonical ones, besides some other books; namely, the Manuscript ζ, contained the Epistles and Gospels; the Manuscripts, ι, ια, ιγ, the Epistles and Acts of the Apostles; and the Manuscripts, δ, ε, θ, the Epistles, Gospels and Acts of the Apostles.

And this any one may gather by noting what Manuscripts the various lections are cited out of, in every book of the New

Teftament. For in the various lections of the canonical Epiftles, and thofe to the Romans, Corinthians, Galatians, Ephefians, Philippians and Coloffians, are found thefe feven Manufcripts, δ, ε, ζ, θ, ι, ια, ιγ, every where cited, and no more than thefe. The fame alfo, and no more are cited in the Epiftles to the Theffalonians, Timothy, Titus, and the Hebrews; one numeral error (whether of the fcribe or typographer) excepted. ⎯Stephens therefore did collect various lections of the epiftles out of only thefe feven Manufcripts, δ, ε, ζ, θ, ι, ια, ιγ, and in all thefe feven, he found the teftimony of " the Three in Heaven " wanting; as you may fee noted in the margin of his edition.

And that this teftimony was wanting in all Stephens's Manufcripts, is apparent alfo by its being generally wanting in the Manufcripts, which are now extant in France. For Father Simon [*] tells us, " That after a " diligent fearch in the library of the King " of France, and in that of Monfieur Colbert, " he could not find it in any one Manufcript;

---

[*] Simon. Critic Hiftory of the New Teft. chap. 18.

" though

"though he consulted seven Manuscripts in
"the King's library, and five in Colbert's".

So then, the authority of the printed books rests only upon the authority of the editions of Erasmus, and Cardinal Ximenes. But seeing that Erasmus omitted it in his two first editions, and inserted it unwillingly against the authority of his Manuscripts in his three last, the authority of these three can be none at all.——When Lee, upon Erasmus putting forth his second edition, fell foul upon him for leaving out the testimony of "the Three in Heaven", Erasmus * answered, "That he had consulted more
"than *seven* Greek Manuscripts, and found it
"wanting in them all, and that if he could
"have found it in any one Manuscript, he
"would have followed *that* in favour of the
"Latin". Hence notice was sent to Erasmus

---

* "Dicam mihi diversis temporibus plura fuisse exem-
"plaria, quam septem, (scilicet Græca) nec in ullo
"horum repertum, quod in nostris (scilicet Latinis) le-
"gitur. Quod si contigisset unum exemplar, in quo
"fuisset, quod nos legimus, nimirum illinc adjecissem,
"quod in cæteris aberat. Id quia non contigit, quod
"solum licuit, feci, indicavi quid in Græcis codicibus
"minus esset". *Hæc Erasmus contra Leum, in hunc locum.*

out of England, that it was in a Manuscript there, and thereupon to avoid ¶ their calumnies, (as he saith) he printed it in his following editions, notwithstanding that he suspected *that* Manuscript to be a new one, corrected by the Latin.

But since, upon enquiry, I cannot learn, that they in England ever heard of any such Manuscript, but from Erasmus; and since he was only told of such a Manuscript in the time of the controversy between him and Lee, and never saw it himself; I cannot forbear to suspect, that it was nothing, but a trick put upon him by some of the popish clergy to try if he would make good what he had offered, the printing of the testimony of "the Three in Heaven", by the

---

¶ " Ex hoc igitur codice Britannico reposuimus; " quod in nostris dicebatur deesse, ne cui sit ansa " calumniandi. Quanquam et hunc suspicor, et La- " tinorum codices, fuisse castigatum. Posteaquam " enim concordiam inierunt cum ecclesiâ Romanâ, " studuerunt et hac in parte cum Romanis consentire".
―――*Erasmi Annotation. in hunc locum Editio tertia*

authority

authority of one Greek copy, and thereby to get it into his edition. ‡

Greek Manuscripts of the scriptures are things of value, and do not use to be thrown away, and such a Manuscript for the testimony of "the Three in Heaven" would have made a greater noise, than the rest have done against it. Let those, who have such a Manuscript, at length tell us, where it is.

So also, let them, who insist upon the edition of Cardinal Ximenes, tell us, by what Manuscripts he printed this testimony; or, at least, where any such Manuscript of good note is to be seen. For, till then, I must take the liberty to believe, that he printed nothing else, than a translation out of the Latin, and that for these reasons.

FIRST. Because in the preface to his edition of the New Testament we are told, that this testimony was printed after Ma-

---

‡ " Versiculus 1. Joan. v. 7. in Syriacâ; ut et ve-
" tustissimis Græcis exemplaribus, nostro Alexandrino,
" aliis manuscriptis Græcis, quos contulimus, non reperitur.———*Walton. Prolegomena.* xiv. 23. *in Bibli. Polyglot.*

nuscripts, taken out of the Pope's library; and these the Cardinal only borrowed ‖ thence, and therefore returned them back, so soon as his edition was finished: And Caryophilus some time after, by the Pope's command, collating the Vatican Manuscripts found the testimony of " the Three in Heaven", wanting in them all. I do not say, but that the Cardinal had other Manuscripts, but these were the chief, and the only ones he thought worth while to tell his reader of

SECONDLY. I startle at the marginal note in this place of the Cardinal's edition. For it is, beside the use of this edition, to put notes in the margin of the Greek text. I have not found it done above thrice in all this edition of the New Testament, and, therefore, there must be something extraordinary, and *that*, in respect of the Greek, because it is in the margin of this text.

" ‑‑‑‑ e Vaticana Romæ Bibliothecâ, bonâ " cum Leonis X pontificis maximi venia" As ‑‑‑‑‑‑‑ his epistle prefixed to the *Quinquage-* ‑‑‑‑‑‑‑ *Psalms*, expresses it.

In

In 1. Corinth xv. There is noted in the margin, a notable variation in the Greek reading ——In Matthew vi. 13. where they, in their edition, recede from the Greek copies, and correct it by the Latin, they make a marginal note, to juſtify their doing ſo.——And ſo here, where the teſtimony of " the Three in Heaven" is generally wanting in the Greek copies, they make a third marginal note, to ſecure themſelves from being blamed for printing it.

Now, in ſuch a caſe as this, there is no queſtion, but they would make the beſt defence; and yet they do not tell of any various lections in their Greek Manuſcripts; nor produce any one Greek Manuſcript on their ſide; but run to the authority of Thomas Aquinas——The Greek Manuſcripts have the text thus. " For there are " Three that bear record, the Spirit, the " Water and the Blood; and theſe Three " are One".——In many of the Latin Manuſcripts, the words, " Theſe Three are " One" are here omitted, and put only at the end of the teſtimony of " the Three " in Heaven", before *that* of " the Spirit, " Water

"Water and Blood"; in others, they are put after both testimonies.

In the Complutensian edition, they follow the former copies, and justify their doing so, by the authority of Thomas Aquinas; § "Thomas, *say they*, in treat-
"ing of *the Three, which bear Witness, in*
"*Heaven*, teaches, that the words, *These*
"*Three are One*, are subjoined for insinua-
"ting the Unity of the essence of the

---

§ The marginal note is this. "Sanctus Thomas
"in expositione secundæ decretalis de summâ Trinitate,
"et Fide Catholica tractans istum passum contra Abba-
"tem Joachim, viz *Tres sunt, qui testimonium dant*
"*in Cœlis, Pater, Verbum, et Spiritus Sanctus*". Dicit
ad literam verba sequentia. "Et ad insinuendam
"Unitatem Trium Personarum subditur, et *Hi Tres*
"*Unum sunt*, Quandoquidem dicitur propter essentiæ
"Unitatem Sed hoc Joachim perverse trahere volens,
"ad Unitatem charitatis et consensus inducebat con-
"sequentem authoritatem. Nam subditur ibidem, *Et*
"*Tres sunt, qui testimonium dant in terrâ, Spiritus*
"*Sanctus, Aqua et Sanguis* Et in quibusdam libris
"additur *Et Hi Tres Unum sunt*. Sed hoc in veris
"exemplaribus non habetur, sed dicitur esse appositum
"ab Hæreticis Arianis ad pervertendum intellectum
"sanum auctoritatis præmissæ de Unitate essentiæ
"Trium Personarum".———*Hæc Beatus Thomas, ubi*
supra.

"Three

" Three Perfons. And whereas, one
" Joachim interpreted this Unity to be only
" in *Love*, and *Confent*, it being thus faid
" of *the Spirit, Water and Blood* in fome
" copies, that *Thefe Three are One*". Thomas replied, " That this laft claufe is not
" extant in the true copies; but was added
" by the Arians for perverting the fenfe".
Thus far this annotation. Now this plainly
refpects the Latin Copies; (for Thomas
underftood not Greek) and therefore part
of the defign of this annotation is to fet right
the Latin reading.

But this is not the main defign. For fo, the annotation fhould have been fet in the margin of the Latin verfion. Its being fet in the margin of the Greek text fhews, that its main defign is to juftify the Greek by the Latin thus rectified and confirmed. Now to make Thomas, thus, in a few words, do all the work, was very artificial; and in Spain, where Thomas is of apoftolical authority, might pafs for a very judicious and fubftantial defence of the printed Greek. But to us, Thomas Aquinas is no Apoftle. We are feeking for the authority of Greek Manufcripts.

(60)

A THIRD reason, why I conceive the Complutensian Greek to have been in this place a translation from the Latin, is, because Stunica, (who, as I told you, was one of the divines employed by the Cardinal in this edition, and at that very time wrote against Erasmus,) when, in his objections, he comes to this text of the testimony of " the Three in Heaven", he cites not one Greek Manuscript for it against Erasmus; but argues wholly from the authority of the Latin.——On the contrary, he sets down, by way of concession, the common reading of the Greek Manuscripts, (as well as his own, and that of others,) in these words: " ὅτι τρεῖς εἰσιν οἱ μαρτυροῦντες τὸ πνεῦμα, καὶ τὸ " ὕδωρ, καὶ τὸ αἷμα· καὶ οἱ τρεῖς εἰς τὸ ἕν εἰσι". And then condemns them all together without exception, and justifies the Latin against them by the authority of Jerome. — " Know, *saith he*, that in this place the
" Greek

— " Sciendum est hoc loco codices apertissime esse
" corruptos, nostros vero veritatem ipsam, ut à primâ
" origine traducti sunt, continere, quod ex prologo B.
" Hieronimi super epistolas manifestè apparet' *Ait*
" *is*, " Quæ si sicut ab eis digestæ sunt, ita quoque ab
" interpretibus

" Greek Manuscripts are most evidently
" corrupted; but ours (that is, the Latin
" ones) contain the truth itself, as they are
" translated from the first original: Which
" is manifest by the prologue of St. Jerome
" upon the Epistles, &c."———And this prologue (which he goes on to cite at length, and of which we gave you an account above) is all he urges in favour of the testimony of " the
" Three in Heaven".

In other places of scripture, where he had Greek Manuscripts on his side, he produces them readily.———So 1. Thessalonians ii. 7. " Ita quidem legitur, *says he*;
" in Græcis codicibus, quos ego viderim".
———In James i. 11. he saith. " Sciendum
" in omnibus Græcis codicibus πορείαις hic
" legi per ει dipthongum".———In 1. Thessalonians v. 23. he saith. " Cum in Græcis
" exemplaribus, quotquot sunt, ὁλόκληρον,
" et in Latinis integer hìc legatur per ne-
" minem discrepantem, nescio, cur Eras-
" mus dixerit, &c."———In Philippians iv.

" interpretibus fideliter in Latinum verterentur elo-
" quium, &c.".———*Hæc Stunica in h. locum Ejus Liber exstat in Criticos*. Vol. IX.

9. " Si quidem in omnibus, *faith he*, Græ-
" cis codicibus; ταυτα λογιζεσθε hìc legitur:
" neque Græci sunt libri, qui πρασσετε hoc
" loco, neque Latini, qui *agite*; nisi men-
" dosos utriusque linguæ codices, cum
" hæc commentaretur Erasmus, per-
" legit".

After this manner, does Stunica produce the Manuscripts used in the Complutensian edition, when they make for him: And here he produces them too, but it is for Erasmus against himself. " Know, *faith* " *he*, that in this place the Greek Manu- " scripts are most evidently corrupted".—— In other places, if he hath but one Manuscript on his side, he produces it magnificently enough; as the Codex Rhodiensis in his discourses upon 2 Corinthians ii. 3. James i. 22. 2 Peter ii. 2. and other texts.

Here he produces all the Manuscripts against himself, without excepting so much as one. And hence Erasmus, in his answer to Stunica, gloried in the consent of the Spanish Manuscripts with his own; and Sanctius Cautanza, another of the Complutensian divines, in his defence of

Stunica,

Stunica, written presently after, had nothing to reply in this point.——Neither could Sepulveda, or the Spanish monks who next undertook the controversy, find one Greek Manuscript, which here made against Erasmus.

Neither had Marchio Valesius better success, though, on that occasion, he collated sixteen Greek Manuscripts, eight whereof belonged to the king of Spain's library; and the other eight to other libraries of Spain: And he did it on purpose to collect out of them, whatever he could meet with in favour of the present vulgar Latin.——Neither did the reprinting of the Complutensian bible by Arias Montanus produce the notice of any such Manuscript, though, on that occasion, many Manuscripts, as well Greek as Latin, fetched from Complutum and other places, were collated by Arias, Lucas Brugensis, Cauter, and others.

So then, to sum up the argument; the Complutensian divines did sometimes correct the Greek by the Latin, without the authority of any Greek Manuscript; as appears by their practice in Matthew vi. 13.

and therefore, their printing the testimony of "the Three in Heaven" is no evidence, that they did it by a Manuscript, but, on the contrary, for want of one, they contented themselves with the authority of Thomas Aquinas: And Stunica confessed, that they had none. Nor has all the Zeal for this text been able since, to discover one, either in Spain, or any where else.

And now you may understand, whence it is, that the Complutensian edition, and the reading of the pretended English Manuscript, set down by Erasmus in his annotations, differ so much from one another. For the Complutensian edition has the text thus: "ὅτι τρεῖς εἰσιν οἱ μαρτυροῦντες ἐν τῷ οὐρανῷ, ὁ πατὴρ, ὁ λόγος, καὶ τὸ ἅγιον πνεῦμα· καὶ οἱ τρεῖς εἰς τὸ ἕν εἰσι. καὶ τρεῖς εἰσιν οἱ μαρτυροῦντες ἐπὶ τῆς γῆς, τὸ πνεῦμα, καὶ τὸ ὕδωρ, καὶ τὸ αἷμα." The pretended English Manuscript thus, "ὅτι τρεῖς εἰσιν οἱ μαρτυροῦντες ἐν τῷ οὐρανῷ, πατὴρ, λόγος, καὶ πνεῦμα· καὶ οὗτοι οἱ τρεῖς ἕν εἰσιν. καὶ τρεῖς μαρτυροῦντες ἐν τῇ γῇ, πνεῦμα, καὶ ὕδωρ, καὶ αἷμα".—The differences are too great to spring from the bare errors of scribes, and arise rather from the

the various translations of the place out of Latin into Greek by two several persons.

But whilst these two readings by their discord confute one another, the readings of the real Greek Manuscripts by their agreement confirm one another, as much. For Caryophilus, who, by the command of pope Urban the Eighth, collated the Vatican, and other Manuscripts, borrowed out of the principal libraries in Rome, found one common reading in them all, without the testimony of " the Three in " Heaven"; as you may see in those his collations, printed in 1673, by Peter Possinus, in the end of his *Catena* of the Greek Fathers upon Mark. He met with eight Manuscripts in all upon the Epistles, and notes their reading thus. " 1. Joan. " v. 7. Manuscripti octo (omnes nempe) " legunt. Ὅτι τρεῖς εἰσιν οἱ μαρτυροῦντες, τὸ " πνεῦμά, καὶ τὸ ὕδωρ, καὶ τὸ αἷμα; καὶ οἱ τρεῖς εἰς " τὸ ἕν εἰσι.------Porro totus septimanus ver- " sus hujus capitis desideratur in octo " Manuscriptis codicibus Græcis, &c." Thus Caryophilus.

The very same reading Erasmus, in his annotations on this place, gives us of all his

Manuscripts, which were more than seven, and so doth Stevens of all his seven, without noting any various lections in them. Only the Comma, which in Stephens's edition is (surely by mistake) set after ὐγανῷ, is to be put in its right place. The very same reading does Stunica also, in his book against Erasmus, note out of the Manuscript, he had seen in Spain, as was shewn above. Nor does Valesius, in his collection of the sixteen Spanish Manuscripts, note any various lections in this text.

The same reading, exactly, have also the Manuscripts in England; namely, that most ancient and most famous one, in the King's library, which was conveyed thither from Ægypt through Greece, and published in Walton's Polyglot Bible; and the four at Oxford, viz. that in New College; and that in Magdalen College; (both very old) and two in Lincoln College: And four or five other ancient ones lately collated at Oxford, in order to a new impression of the Greek testament, as I am informed.

The very same reading have also the three Manuscripts of Monsieur Petavius Gachon, a senator of Paris, whose various lections,

lections, collected by his son, John Gachon, were printed in the Oxford edition of the New Testament, Anno Christi, 1675.---The same reading, without any variation, is published by Francis Asulan in his edition, printed Anno Christi, 1518, by Aldus at Venice out of the Manuscripts of those parts.------The same reading, Oecumenius six hundred years ago found in the Manuscripts of Greece; as you may see in the text of his commentary on this Epistle of St. John.------The same reading also, Cyril of Alexandria met with in the Manuscripts of Egypt, above eleven hundred years ago; as you may see in his citations of the text; both in his Thesaurus, Lib. xiv. cap. 5. And in his first book *De Fide ad Reginas*; excepting that in the latter of these two citations, the particle " εἰς" is omitted; and " μαρτυρῶσι", written for " οἱ μαρτυροῦντες".------And that the very same reading was also in the Manuscripts of the first ages, may be gathered from the conformity of this reading to all the ancient versions.

It may be seen by what has hitherto been said, that this testimony is not to be found in the Greek Manuscripts. Epa-

northotes, ‡ whom Lucas Brugenſis deſcribes to be an ancient, accurate, full, and induſtrious collater of Manuſcripts, found it wanting in all thoſe he met with. " Epa-
" northotes, *ſaith Lucas*, deeſſe hæc eadem
" Græcis libris, et antiquis Latinis anno-
" tat".

Nor have other Collaters made a further diſcovery to this day. Lee, Stunica, and the reſt in England, Spain, Flanders, France and Italy, who conſpired againſt

---

‡ " Habuimus ab Hunnæo id quod maximi facimus
" MS B.bl. correctorium ab incerto auctore, quem
" Epanorthotem, aut correctorem fere vocamus magnâ
" diligentia, ac fide contextum, feculo uti oportet
" antiquos noſtræ editionis codices, eoſque cum Hæ-
" bræ Græc et veterum patrum commentariis ſedulo
" collatos qui liber ad Geneſin, viii. 7. latius à nobis
" deſcriptus eſt." Hæc Lucas, qui ad Geneſin, viii. 7.
ait " Hunc librum multis annis ſcriptum, et
" pluribus fortè compoſitum". Dein loco ex eo
citato pergit. " Ad quæ dici poſſit? An quod libro
" fidem non ſit? Non hoc dicet, qui evolverit,
" namque à noſtri ſeculi ſcriptoribus ex MSS
codicibus collectæ ſunt variæ lectiones omnes prope-
modum in eo comperimus; et ad fontes fideliter
" examinatas deprehendimus" ------*Scripſit hæc Lucas,*
An. 1579 unde ſequitur correctorium ante diſputationes
Eraſ. de Teſtibus in Cœlo elaboratum eſſe.

Eraſmus,

Erasmus, could find nothing in the Manuscripts of those parts against him; if that Phœnix be excepted, which once appeared to somebody somewhere in England; but could never since be seen. Hesselius, * about the year 1565, professor of divinity at Lovain, in his commentary on this place, ingenuously confesses it wanting in all the Greek Manuscripts then known, except two; the one in Spain, the other in England, meaning those, by which the Complutensian divines, and Erasmus printed it. Which two we have shewn to be none at all: unless some Annius dug up one in England. Since that time nothing further has been produced, besides the imaginary books of dreaming Beza.

---

* " Hesselius in hunc locum ait. " Manuscripti
" Græci fere omnes sic se habent. *Quoniam Tres sunt,*
" *qui testimonium dant in terrâ, Spiritus, Aqua et San-*
" *guis, et Hi Tres Unum sunt*, nullâ factâ mentione
" triplicis testimonii de Cœlo, *Patris, Verbi et Spiritus*
" *Sancti*". Dein codices aliter legentes describendo sic
pergit. " Nostro tempore duo Græci codices Manu-
" scripti reperti sunt, unus in Angliâ et alter in His-
" paniâ. quorum uterque hoc loco testimonium habet
" *Patris, Verbi* et *Spiritus Sancti*".

And yet I will not say, but that it may hereafter be found in some Greek copies. For in the Times of the holy war, the Latins had much to do in the East. They were long united to the Greek Church. They made Latin Patriarchs of Jerusalem and Antioch. They reigned at Constantinople over the Greeks from the year, 1204, for above fifty years together: and during this their kingdom, in the year 1215, was assembled the Lateran council, consisting of four hundred and fifteen Bishops; Greeks and Latins together; and therein, the testimony of " the Three in Heaven" was quoted out of some of the Latin Manuscripts, as we told you above. All which might occasion some Greeks, as well as Latins, to note it in the margins of their books; and thence insert it into the text in transcribing.

For this is most certain, that some Greek Manuscripts have been corrected by the Latin ones. Such a book Erasmus † tells us,

---

† " Hic obiter illud incidit admonendum esse Græ-
 " corum aliquot Novi Testamenti codices ad Latina
 " exemplaria

us, that he " Once met with; and that there " was such another in the Pope's library".------He suspected also, that the book in England, out of which he printed the testimony of " the Three in Heaven", was of the same kind, though, I rather think, it was none at all; unless any body were at the pains to transcribe one or two of St. Paul's Epistles.

Such another book was one of those, out of which Valesius collected his *various lections*. Whence Mariana, into whose hands the Manuscript book of those *lections* fell, tells us, that for that reason, in his annotations on the New Testament, he used those *lections* but sparingly and cautiously. And that Valesius did meet with such a

---

" exemplaria emendatos. Id factum est in foedere
" Græcorum cum Romanâ ecclesiâ· Quod foedus
" testatur *Bulla*, quæ dicitur *aurea*. Visum est enim
" et hoc ad firmandam concordiam pertinere. Et nos
" olim in hujusmodi codicem incidimus; et talis adhuc
" dicitur adservari in Bibliothecâ Pontif.------Verum ex
" his corrigere nostros est Lesbiam, ut aiunt, admovere
" regulam".------*Erasmus ad Lectorem. Editio* 5ta *Novi Testamenti.*

corrected Manuscript appears by the lections themselves.

For in the Apocalypse xviii. 17. where the Greek reads " ἐπὶ τόπον"; and the Latin translates *in locum*, and by the error of one letter *in lacum*, as the books now have it; some Grecian has here corrected this book by the Latin, and written " ἐπὶ " λίμνη"; as it is in the lections of Valesius, taken out of this.—— Again in the Apocalypse ix. 11. where the Latin Translation, in expounding the names, *Abaddon et Apollyon*, adds, " Et Latinè habens nomen " exterminans"; Valesius notes the reading in his Greek copy to be, " ῥομφαίᾳ ἔχων " ὄνομα ἐξτερμινανς", which certainly is a translation of the Latin. —— Again, in the Apocalypse xxi. 12. where the Greek has " ἀγγέλους", and some ancient Latin copies, *angelos*, but the far greater part of the Latin copies at present have *angulos*. Valesius, in his Manuscript, reads " γωνίας".—— So in the Apocalypse xix. 6. where the Greek is " ὄχλου πολλοῦ"; the Latin *turbæ magnæ*; and in the later copies, *tubæ magnæ*, Valesius in his Manuscript, reads " σάλπιγγος " — In Hebrews xiii. 2. For " ἔλαθόν",

" ἔλαθόν" *latuerunt*; and in later copies, *placuerunt*, Valesius reads " ἤρεσαν", and in 1. Peter iii. 8. For " τὸ δὲ τέλος", *in fine*; and by an error *in fide*, Valesius reads, " ἐν τῇ " πίστει δὲ". These and such like instances put the thing out of dispute.

Now, though Valesius found not the testimony of " the Three in Heaven" in this Manuscript; and Erasmus tells us, that he never saw it in any Greek Manuscript, and, by consequence, not in that corrected one, which fell into his hands; yet it may have crept out of the Latin into some other books, not yet taken notice of; and even in some Manuscripts, which, in other places, have not been corrected by the Latin, it may possibly have been inserted by some of the Greek Bishops of the Lateran Council, where the testimony of " the Three in " Heaven" was read.------And therefore he, that shall hereafter meet with it in any book, ought, first, before he insist upon the authority of that book, to examine, whether it has not been corrected by the Latin; and whether it be ancienter than the Lateran Council, and Empire of the Latins in Greece; for, if it be liable to either of these

two

two exceptions, it can signify nothing to produce it.

Having given you the History of the controversy, I shall now confirm all, that I have said from the sense of the text itself. For, without the testimony of " the Three " in Heaven", the sense is good and easy, as you may see by the following paraphrase inserted in the text in a different character.

"WHO IS HE, THAT OVERCOMETH
" THE WORLD; BUT HE, THAT BELIEV-
" ETH, THAT JESUS IS THE SON OF
" GOD, *that Son spoken of in the Psalms,*
" *where he saith, Thou art my Son; this*
" *day have I begotten thee.* THIS IS HE,
" THAT, *after the Jews had long expected*
" *him,* CAME, *first in a mortal body* BY
" Baptism of WATER, AND *then in an*
" *immortal one by shedding his* BLOOD;
" *being the Son of God, as well by his*
" *resurrection from the dead;* (Acts xiii.
" 33.) *as by his supernatural birth of the*
" *Virgin,* (Luke i 35.) AND IT IS THE
" SPIRIT *also,* THAT, *together with the*
" *Water and Blood,* BEARETH WITNESS
" *of the truth of his coming;* BECAUSE
" THE

(75)

"THE SPIRIT IS TRUTH; and so a fit and
"unexceptionable witness.

"FOR THERE ARE THREE, THAT BEAR
"RECORD of his coming, THE SPIRIT,
"which he promised to send; and which
"was since shed forth upon us in the form
"of cloven tongues, and in various gifts;
"THE Baptism of WATER, wherein God
"testified, *This is my beloved Son*; AND THE
"shedding of his BLOOD, accompanied
"with his resurrection, whereby he became
"the most faithful martyr, or witness of
"this truth. AND THESE THREE, the
"Spirit, the Baptism, and Passion of Christ;
"AGREE IN witnessing ONE, and the same
"thing; (namely, that the Son of God is
"come) and, therefore, their evidence is
"strong: For the law requires, but two
"consenting witnesses, and here we have
"Three: AND IF WE RECEIVE THE
"WITNESS OF MEN, THE threefold WIT-
"NESS OF GOD, which he bare of his
"Son, by declaring at his baptism; *This is*
"*my beloved Son*; by raising him from the
"dead, and by pouring out his Spirit on us;
"IS GREATER; and therefore ought to be
"more readily received".

Thus

Thus is the sense plain and natural, and the argument full and strong: but, if you insert the testimony of " the Three in " Heaven", you interrupt and spoil it. For the whole design of the Apostle being here to prove to men by witnesses the truth of Christ's coming, I would ask, how the testimony of " the Three in Heaven" makes to this purpose.

If their testimony be not given to men, how does it prove to them the truth of Christ's coming? If it be, how is the testimony in Heaven distinguished from *that* on Earth? It is the same Spirit, which witnesses in Heaven and in Earth. If, in both cases, it witnesses to us men, wherein lies the difference between its witnessing in Heaven, and its witnessing in Earth? If, in the first case, it does not witness to men, to whom doth it witness? And to what purpose? And how does its witnessing make to the design of St. John's discourse? Let them make good sense of it, who are able. For my part I can make none.

If it be said, that we are not to determine, what is scripture, and what not by our private judgment, I confess it in places not controverted,

troverted; but in disputable places, I love to take up with what I can best understand. It is the temper of the hot and superstitious part of mankind, in matters of religin, ever to be fond of misteries, and for that reason, to like best, what they understand the least. Such men may use the Apostle St. JOHN, as they please; but I have that honour for him, as to believe, that he wrote good sense; and therefore take that sense to be *His*, which is the best.

Especially, since I am defended in it by so great authority. For I have on my side the authority of the Fourth General Council, and (so far as I know) that of all the Churches in all Ages, except the modern Latin, and such others, as have lately been influenced by them; and *that* also of all the old versions, and Greek Manuscripts, and ancient Latin ones: And nothing against me, but the authority of Jerome, and the credulity of his followers.

For to tell us of other Manuscripts, without ever letting us know in what libraries they are to be seen: To pretend Manuscripts, which, since their first discovery, could never be heard of; nor were then seen by
persons,

perſons, whoſe names and credit we know, is plainly to impoſe upon the learned world, and ought not to paſs any longer for plain dealing.

The Spaniards tell us plainly, that they followed the Latin, and by the authority of St. Thomas Aquinas left out the Clauſe, " And theſe Three are One", in the eighth verſe, as inſerted by the Arians. And yet St. Ambroſe, St. Auſtin, Eucherius and other Latins, in the Arian age, gathered the Unity of the Deity from this Clauſe; and the omiſſion of it is now, by printing it, acknowledged to be an erroneous correction. The Manuſcript in England wanted the ſame Clauſe, and therefore was a corrected one, like the Spaniſh edition, and the Manuſcript of Valeſius.

Eraſmus, who printed the triple teſtimony in Heaven by that Engliſh Manuſcript, and never ſaw it, tells us, that it was a new one, ſuſpected its ſincerity, and accuſed it publickly in his writings on ſeveral occaſions, for ſeveral years together; and yet his adverſaries in England never anſwered his accuſation, never endeavoured to ſatisfy him, and the world about it: Did not ſo much

as

as let us know, where the record might be confulted for confuting him: but, on the contrary, when they had got the Trinity into his edition, threw by their Manufcript, (if they had one) as an almanack out of date.

And, can fuch fhuffling dealings fatisfy confidering men? Let Manufcripts at length be produced, and freely expofed to the fight of the learned world; but let fuch Manufcripts be produced, as are of authority, or elfe, let it be confeffed, that whilft Jerome pretended to correct the Latin by the Greek, the Latins have corrected both the Latin and the Greek by the fole authority of Jerome.

THE SECOND LETTER:

CONTAINING A

DISSERTATION,

UPON THE

FIRST of TIMOTHY iii. 16.

THE SECOND LETTER:

CONTAINING

A DISSERTATION upon the First of Timothy. iii. 16.

Verſe 16. " Καὶ ὁμολογουμένως μέγα ἐςὶ τὸ
" τῆς εὐσεβείας μυςήριον· ΘΕΟΣ ἐφανερώθη ἐν
" σαρκὶ, ἐδικαιώθη ἐν πνεύματι, ὤφθη ἀγΓέλοις,
" ἐκηρύχθη ἐν ἔθνεσιν, ἐπιςεύθη ἐν κόσμῳ, ἀνελήφθη
" ἐν δόξῃ".

ENGLISH VERSION.

1. Timothy iii. 16.

Verſe 16. " And without controverſy,
" great is the Miſtery of Godlineſs: GOD
" was manifeſt in the Fleſh, juſtified in the
" Spirit, ſeen of Angels, preached unto the
" Gentiles, believed on in the world, re-
" ceived up into Glory".

S I R,

WHAT the Latins have done to the Text of the First Epistle of Saint JOHN, v. 7. the Greeks have done to that of St. Paul's First Epistle to TIMOTHY, iii. 16. For by changing ὅ into ΘC, the Abbreviation of Θεὸς, they now read, " Great is the " Mistery of Godliness: GOD was mani- " fest in the Flesh". Whereas all the Churches for the first four or five hundred years, and the authors of all the ancient versions, Jerome, as well as the rest, read,
" Great

"Great is the Miſtery of Godlineſs, which was manifeſted in the Fleſh".

For this is the common reading of the Ethiopic, Syriac, and Latin Verſions to this day; Jerome's Manuſcripts having given him no occaſion to correct the old vulgar Latin in this Place. Grotius adds the Arabic; but the Egyptian Arabic Verſion has Θεὸς; and ſo has the abovementioned Sclavonian Verſion of Cyrillus. For theſe two Verſions were made long after the ſixth Century, wherein the Corruption began.

With the ancienter verſions agree the writers of the firſt five Centuries, both Greeks and Latins. For they, in all their diſcourſes to prove the Deity of the Son, never alledge this text, (as I can find) as they would all have done; (and ſome of them frequently,) had they read " GOD was " manifeſt in the Fleſh" and therefore they read ὅ. Tertullian *(adverſus Praxeam)* and Cyprian *(adverſus Judeos)* induſtriouſly cite all the places, where CHRIST is called GOD; but have nothing of this.------Alexander of Alexandria, Athanaſius, the Biſhops of the Council of Sardica, Epiphanius, Baſil,

Gregory Nazienzen, Gregory Nyſſen, Chryſoſtom, Cyril of Jeruſalem, Cyril of Alexandria; and amongſt the Latins, Hilary, Lucifer, Jerome, Ambroſe, Auſtin, Phæbedius, Victorinus Afer, Fauſtinus Diaconus, Pope Leo the Great, Arnobius Junior, Cerealis, Vigilius Tapſenſis, Fulgentius, wrote all of them in the fourth and fifth Centuries for the Deity of the Son, and incarnation of God, and ſome of them largely, and in ſeveral tracts, and yet I cannot find, that they ever alledge this text to prove it.

In all the times of the hot and laſting Arian controverſy, it never came into play; though now, that thoſe diſputes are over, they, that read " GOD was manifeſt in the Fleſh", think it one of the moſt obvious, and pertinent texts for the buſineſs.

The Churches therefore of thoſe ages were abſolute ſtrangers to this reading. For, on the contrary, their writers, as often as they have occaſion to cite the reading then in uſe, diſcover that it was ὅ. For though they cite it not to prove the Deity of the Son, yet in their commentaries, and ſometimes in their other diſcourſes they produce it.

it. And particularly Ambrose, or whoever of his Cotemporaries was the author of the commentary on the epistles, reads ὅ; and so doth St. Austin *in Genesin ad literam*, Lib. V.------And Bede in his commentary on this text, where he cites the reading of St. Austin, and the author of the commentary on the epistles ascribed to Jerome.

So also do Primasius and Sedulius in their commentaries on this text; and Victorinus Afer, *Libro primo adversus Arium*; and Idacius Clarus, or rather Vigilius Tapsensis, *Libro tertio, adversus Varimadum, capite* 12. ------And so did Pope Leo the Great, *Epist.* xx. *ad Flavianum*; and Pope Gregory the Great, *Libro* xxxiv. *Moral. cap.* 7. *alias* 4. ------These ancient Latins all cite the text after this manner, " Great is the Mistery of " Godliness, *which* was manifest in the " Flesh"; as the Latin Manuscripts of St. Paul's Epistles generally have it to this day: And therefore, it cannot be doubted, but that this hath been the constant publick reading of the Latin Churches from the beginning.

So also one of the Arians in a homily, printed in Fulgentius's works, reads ὅ, and interprets it of the Son of God, who was born of the Father *ante secula*; and of the virgin, *in novissimo tempore*: and Fulgentius, in his answer to this homily, found no fault with the Citation; but, on the contrary, in his first book to Trasimundus, chap. 6, seems to have read, and understood the text after the same manner, with the other Latins.

Now for the Greeks, I find indeed, that they have changed the ancient reading of the text, not only in the Manuscripts of St. Paul's Epistles; but also in other authors; and yet there are still remaining sufficient Instances among them of what the reading was at first.

Thus, in Chrysostom's commentary on this Epistle, they have now gotten Θεὸς into the text; and yet by considering the commentary by itself, I am satisfied, that he read ὅ. For he neither in his commentary, nor any where else infers the Deity of Christ from this text, nor expounds it, as they do, who read Θεὸς, but with the Latins, who read ὅ, understands by it Christ incarnate; or as he expresses it, " Man made God, and God made Man", and so leaves it at liberty to be taken for either God or Man.------

And

And accordingly in one place of his commentary, he faith. "Ἐφανερώθη ἐν σαρκὶ ὁ δημιεργός". ——— In another place; "Ἄνθρωπος ὤφθη ἀναμάρτητος, ἄνθρωπος ἀνελήφθη ἐκηρύχθη ἐν κόσμῳ μεθ' ἡμῶν εἶδον αὐτὸν οἱ ἄγγελοι". "Man appeared without Sin; Man was received up, Man was preached in the world; was seen amongst us by Angels". Instead of "ὁ ἐφανερώθη ἐν σαρκὶ ἐδικαιώθη ἐν πνεύματι", &c. he faith, "Man appeared without Sin; Man was received up, was preached in the world, was seen amongst us by Angels"; making *Man* the Nominative Case to these, and all the Verbs which follow; which certainly he would not have done, had Θεὸς been their Nominative Case expresly in the text. He might properly put man for ὁ', but not for Θεὸς. Neither could he have put ἀναμάρτητος for ἐδικαιώθη; if he had read in his text, θεὸς ἐδικαιώθη. For what man of common sense would say, that God was made sinless in and through the Spirit.

But what I have said of Chrysostom will be more evident, when I shall have shewn you, how afterwards, in the time of the Nestorian controversy, all parties read ὁ without

out any dispute raised about the reading; and how the Greeks have since corrupted the text in Cyril's writings, and changed ὁ into ὅς, as they have done in Chrysostom's

And *first*, that the Nestorians read ὁ is evident by some fragments of the orations or homilies of Nestorius sent by him to the Pope, and cited by Arnobius Junior, in the second book of his conflict with Serapion. For there, in order to shew what was the opinion of Nestorius, and how he defended it, he cites two of his orations in these words. " Non peperit sanctissima Maria
" Deitatem; nam quod natum est de carne,
" caro est. Non peperit creatura Creato-
" rem; sed peperit hominem Deitatis mi-
" nistrum. Non ædificavit Deum, Ver-
" bum, Spiritus Sanctus; quod ex ipsâ na-
" tum est, de Spiritu Sancto est. Deo ita-
" que virgo templum ex virginea ædifica-
" vit. Et paulo post, " Qui per se natus
" est Deus in utero (scilicet ante Lucipho-
" rum) Deus est". ------ Et paulo post.
" Servi formam in Deo honoramus". Et
" alia prædicatione; " Spiritum divina
" generat natura, qui humanitatem ejus
" creavit. Quicquid ex Mariâ natum est,
" de

"de Spiritu Sancto est, qui et secundum
"justitiam replevit, quod creatum est; hoc
"quod manifestatum est in carne, justifica-
"tum est in Spiritu". Which last words in the language, wherein Nestorius wrote those homilies, are, "ὃ ἐφανερώθη ἐν σαρκὶ,
"ἐδικαιώθη ἐν πνεύματι".

Here you see, that Nestorius reads ὃ expresly; not only so, but absolutely excludes God from being understood by it; arguing, that the virgin was not Θεοτόκος; because that thing, which was manifested in the Flesh, was justified in the Spirit; or (as he expounds it) replenished by the Spirit in righteousness; and calling that thing, which was manifested in the Flesh, a Creature. "Spiritus,
"*saith he*, secundum justitiam replevit [hoc]
"quod creatum est; [nempe] hoc quod ma-
"nifestatum est in carne, justificatum est in
"Spiritu".

And now whilst he read the text after this manner, and urged it thus against the Deity of Christ, one would expect, that if this had not been the received publick reading in the Greek Churches, his adversaries would have fallen foul upon him, and exclaimed against him for falsifying the text, and blasphemously saying, it was a created thing,

thing, which the scripture calls *God manifested in the Flesh*. And such an accusation, as this, would surely have made as great a noise, as any thing else in the controversy.

And yet I meet with nothing of this kind in history. His adversaries do not so much as tell him, that Θεὸς was in the text. They were so far from raising any controversy about the reading, that they do not in the least correct him for it, but, on the contrary, they themselves in their answers to his writings read ὃ, as he did; and they only laboured by various disputations to put another sense upon the text; as I find by Cassian and Cyril, the two principal, who at that time wrote against him.

John Cassian was Chrysostom's Scholar, and his Deacon and Legate to the Pope, and after the banishment of Chrysostom, retired from Constantinople into Syria and Egypt, where he lived a monastick life for some time, and then ended his days in France. At that time, therefore, when Nestorius, who was Patriarch of Constantinople, broached his opinion, and Cyril, the Patriarch of Alexandria opposed him; Nestorius sent a

legacy

legacy to Rome with copies of his orations to let the Pope understand the controversy; and thereupon Leo, the Great, who was then Archdeacon of the Church of Rome, and afterwards Pope, put Caſſian (then in France) upon writing his book, *De incarnatione Domini*, againſt Neſtorius. He wrote it therefore, in the year of our Lord 430; as Baronius alſo reckons. For he wrote it before the condemnation of Neſtorius in the Council of Epheſus; as appears by the book itſelf.

This book is now extant only in Latin; but conſidering, that his deſign in writing was to ſtir up the Greek Church againſt Neſtorius, and that too, for the making great impreſſion upon them, he quotes Greek fathers at the end of his book, and concludes with an exhortation to the Citizens of Conſtantinople, telling them, that, what he wrote, he had received from his maſter Chryſoſtom; I am ſatisfied, that he wrote it originally in Greek. His other books were in both languages. For Photius ſaw them in eloquent Greek; and it is more likely, that they had their author's eloquent language from their author, and the Latin

from

from one of the Latins, where he lived; than that the contrary should be true.

Now in this treatise * when he comes to consider the passage of Nestorius about this text, of which we gave you an account above, out of Arnobius, he returns this answer to it. " Jam primum enim hoc quod ais (Nestori) " quia justitiâ repleverit, quod creatum est; " et hoc apostolico vis testimonio comprobare, " quod dicat, *apparuit in carne; justificatus* " *est in Spiritu*; utrumque insano sensu, et " furioso Spiritu loqueris. Quia et hoc, " quod à Spiritu vis eum repletum esse justi- " tiâ, ideo ponis, ut ostendas ejus vacuita- " tem cui præstitam esse asseras justitiæ ad " impletionem. Et hoc, quod super hâc re " apostolico testimonio uteris, divini testi- " monii ordinem rationemque furaris. Non " enim ita ab apostolo positum est, ut tu id " truncatum, vitiatumque posuisti. Quid " enim apostolus ait ? *Et manifestè magnum* " *est pietatis sacramentum, quod manifestatum* " *est in carne, justificatum est in Spiritu.* Vides " ergo, quod misterium pietatis, vel sacra- " mentum justificatum apostolus prædicavit".

---

* " Libro septimo, capite 18".

------Thus

------Thus far Cassian is not only reading ὅ, but confuting Nestorius by that reading. ------For whereas Nestorius said it was a Creature, which was justified, Cassian tells him, that if he had read the whole text, he would have found, that it was *The Mystery of Godliness*. " Vides ergo, *saith he*, quod " misterium pietatis justificatum apostolus " prædicavit". He does not say. " Deum " justificatum apostolus prædicavit". (As he would certainly have done, had that been in his Bible); but *misterium*; and so makes *misterium*, or which is all one, its relative *quod*, the Nominative Case to the Verbs that follow.

In another part of this treatise, *Libro quinto* cap. 12. Cassian cites, and interprets the text, as follows. " Et manifestè " magnum est pietatis sacramentum, *quod* " manifestatum est in carne, justificatum, " &c. Quod ergo magnum est illud sacra- " mentum quod manifestatum est in carne? " Deus, scilicet, natus in carne, Deus visus " in corpore, qui utique sicut palam est " manifestatus in carne, ita palam est as- " sumptus in gloriâ".------So you see Nestorius and Cassian agree in reading ὅ; but
differ

differ in interpreting it; the one restraining it to a Creature, by reason of its being justified; the other restraining it to God, by reason of its being a great mistery, and assumed in glory.

In like manner Cyril, the great adversary of Nestorius, in his three books, *De Fide ad Imperatorem et Reginas*, written against him in the beginning of the controversy, did not reprehend him; as if he had cited the text falsely; but only complained of his misinterpreting it; telling him that he did not understand the *Mistery of Godliness*; and that it was not a *created thing* (as he thought) but the Word or Son of God; and arguing for this interpretation from the circumstances of the text.

And first, in his book, *De Fide ad Imperatorem*, Sect. 7. he has this passage. " Πλα-
" νᾶσθε, μὴ εἰδότες τὰς γραφὰς· μήτε μέν τὸ
" μέγα τῆς εὐσεβείας μυτήριον, τυτέςι Χριςὸν
" ὃς ἐφανερώθη ἐν σαρκὶ, ἐδικαιώθη ἐν πνεύματι,
" &c." " Ye err, *saith he,* not knowing
" the scriptures; nor the Mistery of God-
" liness, that is, CHRIST, who was manifest-
" ed in the Flesh, justified in the Spirit."
------By this citation, it is plain, that he read ὃ. For by putting Χριςὸν, for μυτήριον, he

he turns ὅ into ὅς; unless you will say, that he turns θεὸς into ὅς, which is very hard.

For had θεὸς been in this text he would not have said μυσήριον, τυτέςι Χριςὸν, ὃς ἐφανερώθη; but μυσήριον, Θεὸς, τυτέςι Χριςὸς ἐφανερώθη, putting Χριςὸς, not for μυσήριον; but for θεὸς. For Χριςὸς and Θεὸς are equipollent: But in making Χριςὸν and μυσήριον equipollent, he makes μυσήριον the Nominative Case to ἐφανερώθη, and therefore read them joined in this text by the article ὅ.------Had he read θεὸς, he would never have left out that authentick and demonstrative word, and by way of interpretation for μυσήριον θεὸς, written Χριςὸν ὅς. For this was not to argue against Nestorius; but to spoil the argument, which lay before him.

Neither would he have gone on, as he does, within a few lines after, to propound it as his opinion, that the Word or Son of God was to be understood by this Mistery, and to dispute for this his opinion out of other Texts of Scripture; as he does after this manner. ‡ " Moreover, saith he,

---

‡ " Ἔτι γὰρ ἂν οὐχ ἕτερον οἶμαι τὶ τὸ τῆς εὐσεβείας
" μυσήριον, ἢ αὐτὸς ἡμῖν ὁ ἐκ θεοῦ πατρὸς λόγος, ὃς ἐφα-
" νερώθη ἐν σαρκί. Γεγέννηται γὰρ διὰ τῆς ἁγίας παρθένυ
" καὶ θεοτόκυ, μορφὴν δούλου λαβών"------Cyril de Fide
ad Imperatorem Sect. 8

H " that

" that Miſtery of Godlineſs, in my opinion,
" is nothing elſe than the very Word of
" God the Father; which for our ſake was
" manifeſted in the Fleſh. For in taking
" the form of a Servant, it was born of the
" holy God-bearing Virgin, &c."------And
then after many other things, he, at length,
in Sections 23 and 24, concludes, that,
" This divine Miſtery is above our under-
" ſtanding, and that the only begotten Son,
" who is God, and, according to the Scrip-
" tures, the Lord of all things, appeared
" to us, was ſeen on earth, and became a
" Man."

Again in the firſt of his two treatiſes, *De Fide ad Reginas*, near the end, he cites the text, and argues thus againſt the interpretation of Neſtorius. " Who is it, ſaith he,
" that is maniſeſted in the Fleſh? Is it not
" fully evident, that it is no other than the
" Word of God the Father? For ſo will it
" be a great Miſtery of Godlineſs (which
" was ‖ manifeſted in the Fleſh): He was

―――――――――――――

‖ Codex Græcus legit ὃς ſenſu perturbato.

" ſeen

" seen of Angels, ascending into Heaven;
" he was moreover preached to the Gen-
" tiles by the holy Apostles; he was believ-
" ed on in the world: But this is not, as a
" mere man, but as God born in the Flesh,
" and after our manner.

So also in his second book, *De Fide ad Reginas*, * he cites the place again, and then argues upon it against the opinion of Nestorius after this manner. " If the Word
" being God is said to become a Man, and
" yet continue what he was before, without
" losing his Deity, the Mistery of Godli-
" ness is without doubt a very great one:
" But if Christ be a mere Man, joined with
" God only in the parity of dignity and
" power (for this is maintained by some
" unlearned men) how is he manifested in
" the Flesh? Is it not plain, that every
" Man is in the Flesh, and cannot other-
" wise be seen by any body; How then
" was he said to be seen of the holy Angels?
" For do they not also see us? What was
" there new or extraordinary in Christ, if

---
* Section 33.

" the Angels saw him such a Man, as we
" are, and nothing more, &c."

Thus Cyril goes on to give his reasons, why that, which was manifested in the Flesh, was not a mere created Man, as Nestorius interpreted; but the eternal Word, or Son of God; all which would have been very superfluous, and impertinent, if θεὸς had then been expresly in the text.

Seeing therefore Nestorius alledged the text to prove, that it was a created thing, which was manifested in the Flesh; and Cyril in confuting him did not answer, that it was God expresly in the text; nor raise any debate about the reading; but only put another interpretation upon the text, than Nestorius had done; arguing with Cassian, that in the text, it was not a mere Man, as Nestorius contended, but a great *Mistery of Godliness*; and by consequence Christ, the Son of God, *which was manifested in the Flesh*; and labouring by divers arguments to prove this interpretation, it is evident beyond all cavil, that Cyril was a stranger to Θεὸς, now got into the text, and read ὅ, as Nestorius and Cassian did

And

And yet in these his books *ad Reginas*, wherever he quotes this text, the Greeks have since corrected it by their corrected Manuscripts of St. Paul's Epistles, and written Θεὸς instead of ὅ; Whence, if you would truly understand the Nestorian history, you must read ὅ for Θεὸς in all Cyril's citations of this text.

Now, whilst Cyril read ὅ, and in the explanation of the *twelve chapters*, or articles, quoted this text in the second article; and this explanation was recited by him in the Council of Ephesus, and approved by the Council †, with an Anathema at the end of every article; it is manifest, that this Council allowed the reading ὅ, and, by consequence, that ὅ was the authentick and public uncontroverted reading, till after the times of this Council.

For if Nestorius and Cyril, the Patriarchs of Constantinople and Alexandria, and the heads of the two parties in this controversy, read ὅ; and their writings went about among the Eastern Churches, and were canvassed by the bishops and clergy without

---

† Concil. Ephef. Par. iii. sub initio.

any dispute raised about the reading, and if Cyril read ὅ by the approbation of the Council itself, I think, that the conclusion we make, of its being then the general uncontroverted reading, must needs be granted us. And if the authority of one of the four first general Councils make any thing for the truth of the matter, or to settle the reading, we have that into the bargain.

Yet, whilst the Nestorian controversy brought the text into play, and the two parties ran the interpretation into extremes, the one disputing that ὅ was a Creature; the other, that it was the Word of God; the prevalence of the latter party made it pass for the orthodox opinion, that ὅ was God; and so gave occasion to the Greeks henceforward to change the language of *Christ* into that of *God*, and say, in their expositions of the text, that *God was manifested in the Flesh* (as I find Theodoret doth) and, at length, to write God in the text itself; the easy change of ὅ into ΘC, (the abbreviation of Θὲς,) inviting them to do it: and if this was become the orthodox authentick reading, to set right the text in Chrysostom, Cyril,

Cyril, Theodoret, and wherever elſe they found it (in their opinion) corrupted by hereticks.

And the man, that firſt began thus to alter the ſacred text, was Macedonius, the Patriarch of Conſtantinople, in the beginning of the ſixth Century. For the Emperor Anaſtaſius baniſhed him for corrupting it.---At that time, the Greek Church had been long divided about the Council of Chalcedon. Many, who allowed the condemnation of Eutyches, rejecting the Council by reaſon of its decreeing, by the influence of the Biſhop of Rome's letter againſt Eutyches, that Chriſt ſubſiſted not only *Ex duabus naturis*, which Eutyches allowed, but alſo, *In duabus naturis*, which language was new to the Greeks; and by a great part of the Church taken for Neſtorianiſm. For they underſtood, that as the *Body* and *Soul* made the Nature of Man; ſo *God* and *Man* made the Nature of *Chriſt*, aſſigning the Nature to the Perſon of Chriſt, as well as to all other things, and not conſidering, that in all compounds the ſeveral parts have alſo their ſeveral Natures.

Hence each party endeavoured to render the other suspected of heresy; as if they, that were for the Council, secretly favoured the Nestorians, and they that were against it, the Eutychians. For one party, in maintaining two distinct Natures in Christ, were thought to deny the Nature of one Person with Nestorius, and the other party, in opposing two distinct Natures in him, were thought to deny the truth of one of the Natures, with Eutyches. Both parties, therefore, to clear themselves of these imputations, anathematised both those heresies; and therefore, whilst they thus differed in their modes of speaking, they agreed in the sense, as Evagrius well observes.

But the Bishops of Rome and Alexandria, being engaged against one another, and for a long time distracting the East by these disputes: At length, the Emperor Zeno, to quiet his empire, and perhaps to secure it from the encroachment of the Bishop of Rome, who, by a verbal contest, * aspired to the name and authority of universal Bishop, sent about an Henoticum, or pacificatory de-

---

* V de Baronium, Anno 451. Sect. 149, 150, 151.

cree, wherein he anathematised both Nestorius and Eutyches with their followers on the one hand, and abrogated the Pope's letter, and the Council on the other: And his successor Anastasius, for the same end, laboured for to have this decree signed by all the Bishops. And Macedonius at first subscribed it; but afterwards heading those, who stood up for the Council * was, for his corrupting the Scriptures in favour of his opinion; and such other things, as were laid to his charge, depofed and banished †, Anno Christi 512.

But his own party (which at length prevailed) defended him, as if oppressed by calumnies; and so received that reading for genuine, which he had put about among them. For how ready are all parties to receive what they reckon on their side, Jerome well knew, when he recommended the testimony of " the Three in Heaven"

---

* Evagrius, Lib. iii. Cap. xxi. 44.
Theodorus Lector, Lib. ii. and Marcellini Cronicon

† Flavian was banished in the year of Antioch 561, as Evagrius notes, and Macedonius was banished the same year, or the year before.

by

by its usefulness, and we have a notable instance of it, in the last age; when the Churches both Eastern and Western received this testimony in a moment, into their Greek Testaments, and still continue with great zeal and passion to defend it for the ancient reading against the authority of all the Greek Manuscripts.

But now I have told you the original of the corruption, I must tell you my author; and he is Liberatus, Arch-deacon of the Church of Carthage, who lived in that very age. For in his Breviary, which he wrote in the year 535, or soon after, and collected (as he saith in his preface) out of Greek records, he delivers it in these words " Hoc
" tempore Macedonius Constantinopolitanus
" Episcopus ab Imperatore Anastasio dicitur
" expulsus, tanquam evangelia falsaret, et
" maxime illud Apostoli dictum. *Quia ap-*
" *paruit in carne, justificatum in Spiritu.*
" Hunc enim mutasse, ubi habet *Qui* . . . . .
" hoc est . . . . . monosyllabum Græcum,
" literá mutatâ in . . . . vertisse et fecisse
"   . id est, ut esset Deus, apparuit
" per carnem Tanquam Nestorianus ergo
                                " expellitur

" expellitur per severum Monachum". §

The Greek Letters here omitted are in the second edition; and in those of the Councils thus inserted: " Ubi habet ὅς, hoc " est, *qui*, monosyllabum Græcum, literâ " mutatâ ο in ω vertisse, et fecisse, ὡς; id " est, ut esset, Deus apparuit per carnem". But this interpolation was surely made by conjecture. For if Θεός was in the sacred text, before the corruption; then ὅς or ὁ was not in, and so could not be changed into ὡς: But if Θεός was not in, it could not be brought in by this change. The interpolation therefore is inconsistent and spurious, and seems to have been occasioned by straining to make out Nestorianism here, the Scribes for that end, ¶ referring the words, *ut esset*,

---

§ Vide Baronii Annal 510. Sect 9.

¶ *Nota bene.* In Hincmari opusculis, cap. 18 cap. 22 the words, *ut esset*, are in like manner referred to the sacred text, and some body, to make out the sense, has in their stead added, *ut appareret*, to the words of Liberatus; and written, *ut appareret, ut esset Deus*, &c. But the words, *ut appareret*, not being in Liberatus must be struck out, and supplied by setting the comma after, *ut esset*, to part these words from the sacred text.

to the sacred text; and then the interpolator writing ὅς for ut. Whereas, they should have referred, *ut esset,* to the words of Liberatus, thus distinguished from the sacred text. "Id est, ut esset, *Deus apparuit per* "*carnem*".

I had rather, therefore, wave the conjecture of this interpolator, and fill up the Lacunæ by the authority of an ancient author, Hincmarus, who above eight hundred years ago * related the fact out of Liberatus, after this manner. " Quidam
" nimirum ipsas scripturas verbis inlicitis
" imposturaverunt; sicut Macedonius
" Constantinopolitanus Episcopus, qui ab
" Anastasio Imperatore, ideo à civitate ex-
" pulsus legitur, quoniam falsavit evangelia;
" et illum Apostoli locum, *Quod apparuit in*
" *carne, justificatum est in Spiritu,* per cog-
" nationem Græcarum literarum O et Θ hoc
" modo mutando falsavit. Ubi enim ha-
" buit, *Qui,* hoc est OC, monosyllabum
" Græcum, literâ mutatâ O in Θ, vertit,
" et fecit ΘC, id est, ut esset, Deus appa-
" ruit per carnem, quâpropter tanquam

---

* Hincmari opuscul Artic. xxxiii. cap. 18.

" Nestorianus

"Neſtorianus fuit expulſus".-------He was baniſhed therefore for changing the ancient reading (which was not OC, as theſe authors have it by miſtake; but ὅ) into ΘC.

But whereas, he is repreſented a Neſtorian, for doing this, the meaning is, that he was baniſhed for corrupting the text in favour of the doctrine of two Natures in Chriſt, which his enemies accounted Neſtorianiſm; though it was not really ſo. Neſtorius held only a human Nature in Chriſt; and that God, *the word*, dwelt in this Nature, as the Spirit in a holy man; and therefore interpreted ὅ of the human Nature. This doctrine Macedonius anathematiſed, and maintained two Natures in Chriſt, and, for proving this, corrupted the text; and made it God, *who was manifeſt in the Fleſh*.------This diſtinguiſhing Chriſt into two Natures was, by the enemies of Macedonius, accounted Neſtorianiſm in other language; and in this reſpect the Hiſtorian ſaith, that they baniſhed him, as a Neſtorian for corrupting the text; though he was not really of the opinion.

But whilſt they tell us, that he was baniſhed, as a Neſtorian for this, without explaining what is here meant by a Neſtorian;

it looks like a trickish way of speaking, used by his friends to ridicule the proceedings against him, as inconsistent; perhaps to invert the crime of falsation, as if a Nestorian would rather change ΘC into O.

For they, that read history with judgment, will too often meet with such trickish reports, and even in the very story of Macedonius, I meet with some other reports of the same kind. For Macedonius, having in his keeping the original acts of the Council of Chalcedon, signed by that Emperor, under whom it was called; and refusing to deliver up this book to the Emperor Anastasius, some, to make this Emperor perjured, distorted the story, as if at his coming to the crown, he had promised under his hand and oath, that he would not act against the Council of Chalcedon, and represented his subscribed promise to be the book, which Macedonius refused to deliver back to him.

Macedonius had got his bishoprick by being against the Council of Chalcedon, and had subscribed the Henoticum * of the Em-

---

* Vide Annotationes Valesii in Evagrii, &c. Lib. iii. Cap. 3

peror

peror Zeno, in which that Council was anathematifed; and this being objected againſt him, his friends, to ſtifle the accuſation, make a contrary ſtory of the Emperor, as if, when he came to the crown, he had done as much as that in behalf of the Council.

Another report was †, " That the people
" of Alexandria, and of all Egypt, great and
" ſmall, bond and free, prieſts and monks,
" excepting only ſtrangers, became about
" this time poſſeſſed with evil ſpirits, and
" being deprived of human ſpeech, barked
" day and night, like dogs; ſo that they
" were afterwards bound with iron chains,
" and drawn to the Church, that they might
" recover their health. For they all eat up
" their hands and arms. And then an Angel
" appeared to ſome of the people, ſaying,
" that this happened to them, becauſe they
" anathematifed the Council of Chalcedon,
" and threatned, that they ſhould do ſo no
" more."

Again, we are told in hiſtory, * " That
" the adverſaries of Macedonius produced

---

† Victor Tununenſis in Chronico.

* Evagrius, Lib. III Cap. 32.

" certain

" certain boys in judgment, to accuſe both
" him, and themſelves of ſodomy, but that
" when they found his genitals were cut off,
" they betook themſelves to other arts for the
" depoſing of him". Now, if you can believe, that a eunuch had the beard and voice of another man; and that in a ſolemn Council, the great Patriarch of the Eaſt was thus accuſed, and thus acquitted, and yet after all depoſed; you muſt acknowledge, that there were many Biſhops among the Greeks, who would not ſtick at, as ill and ſhameleſs things, as corrupting the Scriptures. But if all this be a ſham, invented to diſcredit the Council; the need of ſuch ſhams adds credit to their proceedings in condemning him for a falſary.

This Council (if I miſtake not) ſat firſt at Conſtantinople, being that Council, which Theodorus calls, " a company of mercenary
" wretches": and Nicephorus; " a conven-
" tion of hereticks, aſſembled againſt Mace-
" donius". Upon their adding to the *
" thrice holy" the words, " who art cruci-

---

* Theodor. Lib. ii —— Nicephor. Lib. xvi. Cap. 26 —— Evagri Lib. iii. Cap. 44.

" fied

"fied for us"; the people fell into a tumult; and afterwards, when Macedonius came to be accused, they fell into a greater tumult, crying out, "The time of persecution is at "hand. Let no man desert the Father", meaning Macedonius.

In this tumult (which was said to be stirred up by the Clergy of Constantinople) many parts of the city were burnt, and the Nobles and Emperor brought into the greatest danger; insomuch, that the Emperor was forced to proffer the resignation of his empire, before he could quiet the multitude. Then seeing, that if Macedonius were judged, the people would defend him, he caused him to be carried by force in the night to Chalcedon; and thence into banishment, as Theodorus writes. Whence I gather, that the Council removed also to Chalcedon, to avoid the tumult, and finish their proceedings there.

For the story of his being accused in judgment by boys, Nicephorus places after this tumult; and all agree, that he was condemned; and the Monks of Palestine, in an Epistle, recorded by Evagrius, say, that

Xenaias

(114)

Xenaias and Dioscorus, joined with many Bishops, banished him. When his condemnation was sent him, signed by the Emperor, he asked, whether they, that had condemned him, received the Council of Chalcedon, and when they, that brought him the sentence, denied it, he replied. " If " Arians and Macedonians had sent me a " book of condemnation, could I receive " it"? So that, it seems, he stood upon the illegality of the Council.

The next day, one Timothy was made Bishop of Constantinople; and he sent about the condemnation of Macedonius to all the absent Bishops to be subscribed *.---Whence, I think, it will be easily granted, that he was condemned, as a falsary, by the greatest part of the Eastern empire; and by consequence, that the genuine reading was till then, by the Churches of that Empire, accounted ὅ.-----For had not the publick reading then been ὅ, there could have been no colour for pretending, that he changed it into ΘC

---

* Theophanes, pag 135

About

About six years after, Anaſtaſius the Emperor died; and his Succeſſors Juſtin and Juſtinian ſet up the authority of the Council of Chalcedon again, together with that of the Pope over the Eaſtern Churches, as univerſal Biſhop; and from that time, the friends of Macedonius prevailing, it is probable, that in oppoſition to the hereticks, which condemned him; and for promoting and eſtabliſhing the doctrine of two Natures in Chriſt, they received and ſpread abroad the reading ΘC. But as for the authority of the Pope, *that* fell again with Rome in the Gothick wars; and ſlept, till Phocas revived it again.

I told you of ſeveral ſhams put about by the friends of Macedonius to diſcredit the proceedings of the Council againſt him. There is one, which notably confirms what has hitherto been ſaid, and makes it plain, that his friends received his corruptions, as genuine Scripture. For whereas Macedonius was baniſhed for corrupting the New Teſtament, his friends retorted the crime upon the Council, as if they had taken upon them, under colour of purging the Goſpels from the corruptions of Macedonius to correct in them, whatever they thought the Apostles, as unskilful men and idiots, had written amiss.

For this I gather from an ironical report of this kind, put about in the West, and thus recorded by Victor Tununensis. "Messala. V. C. Consulibus, Constantino-"poli, jubente Anastasio Imperatore, sancta "evangelia, tanquam ab idiotis composita re-"prehenduntur, et emendantur", that is, "In the Consulship of Messala the holy Gos-"pels, by the command of the Emperor "Anastasius, were censured and corrected "at Constantinople, as if written by evan-"gelists, that were idiots". Here Victor errs in the year. For Messala was Consul, Anno Christi 506, that is, six years before the banishment of Macedonius. But Victor is very uncertain in dates of the years. For he places the banishment of Macedonius in the Consulship of Arienus, Anno Christi 502; and the above-mentioned tumult about the Trisagium, in the Consulship of Probus, Anno Christi 513; whereas all these things happened in the same year.

For

For it is plain by this chronicle, that the Scriptures were examined and corrected about this time by a Council at Constantinople by the order of Anastasius; and I meet with no other Council, to which this character can agree; besides that which deposed Macedonius. Now, that they should censure and correct the Gospels, as if written by ideots, is too plainly ironical, to be truly history; and therefore it must be an abusive report put about to discredit the Council.

So then the falsation was set on foot in the beginning of the fifth Century, and is now of about twelve hundred years standing; and therefore, since it lay but in a letter; and so was more easily spread abroad in the Greek Manuscripts, then the testimony of "the Three in Heaven", in the Latin ones, we need not wonder, if the old reading be scarce to be met with, in any Greek Manuscripts, now extant; and yet it is in some.

For though Beza tells us, that all the Greek Manuscripts read Θεός; yet, I must tell Beza's readers, that all his Manuscripts read ὅ. For he had no other Manuscripts

(118)

on the Epistles, besides the Claromontan; and in this Manuscript, as Morinus by ocular inspection has since informed us, the ancient reading was ὅ, * but yet, in another hand, and with other ink, the letter Θ has been written out of the line; and the letter Ο (omicron) thickened to make a C (a sigma) appears: which instance shews sufficiently, by whom the ancient reading has been changed.

Valesius also reads ὅ in one of the Spanish Manuscripts †, and so did the authors of the

---

* "Alia manu, et atramento extra lineæ seriem addita est litera Θ, et ambesâ paululum Ο, ut appareret sigma Sed præpostera emendatio facile conspicitur". *Hou. . . . in . . . ratioribus Biblicis. Lib. 1. Exercitat. . . cap. 4.*——At Beza nobis aliquod invidit, ut ex ejus e . . . ad Academiam Cantabrigiensem a Waltono editam liquet, ab. variantes aliquas lectiones celandas esse ad . . .

† These Spanish Manuscripts, that have been several times mentioned in these letters, and which Sir Isaac (as well as many others) apprehended to be Greek ones, collated by Valesius, were really Latin ones. The Ma. . . . no other, but then he translated the various readings into Greek, which imposed upon many of the learned, but it is much to be wondered, that it should escape the penetration of this great man.

Oxford

(119)

Oxford edition of the New Teſtament, Anno Chriſti, 1675, read it in the Manuſcript of Lincoln College Library, which is the oldeſt of the Oxford Manuſcripts.----So then, there are ſome of the ancient Greek Manuſcripts, which read ὅ; but I do not hear of any Latin ones, either ancient or modern, which read Θεὸς.

And beſides, to read Θεὸς makes the ſenſe obſcure and difficult. For how could it properly be ſaid, " that God was juſtified by " the Spirit"? But to read ὅ, and interpret it of Chriſt, as the ancient Chriſtians did; without reſtraining it to his divinity, makes the ſenſe very eaſy. For the promiſed and long expected Meſſias, the hope of Iſrael, is to us, " the great Miſtery of Godlineſs". And this miſtery was at length manifeſted to the Jews from the time of his Baptiſm, and juſtified to be the perſon, whom they expected.

I have now given you an account of the corruption of * * *

ADVER-

ERRATA.

Page 71, Line 9. For *Paul's*, read *John's*.
P. 77, l. 4. for *Religin*, read *Religion*.

ADVERTISEMENT

OF THE

EDITOR.

"THE Manuscript is defective in the
"end of the Second Letter; neither
"can it be absolutely determined, how much
"of it has been *lost*. However, it is most
"probable, that very little of it is wanting;
"and though the Reader will be sorry to find
"himself deprived even of a few lines, that
"have dropt from the pen of so great a Man,
"he cannot have sustained the loss of any
"matter, which will at all affect the point
"in debate. Sir Isaac having given his
"proofs,

" proofs, that the prefent reading of the
" GREEK MANUSCRIPTS in general, and of
" all our printed books, could not be the
" ancient and *true one*, in this paffage, 1 *Tim.*
" ii 16. and afterwards pointed out the
" caufe of this corruption of the Text; as
" well as the time when, and the perfon by
" whom, it was fo corrupted; and, laftly,
" having fhewn, that the change made in
" it has rendered the fenfe of the paffage
" obfcure, difficult and hardly proper, which
" was otherwife eafy and clear, from thefe
" confiderations, it is more than probable,
" that the Author was concluding with an
" application fomewhat fimilar to that we
" find at the end of the FORMER LETTER,
" efpecially fince he has begun the broken
" paragraph at the end, with a general re-
" capitulation of what he had done.

" The Reader is to be informed, that the
" MANUSCRIPT of thefe TWO LETTERS is
" ftill preferved in the Library of the RE-
" MONSTRANTS in *Holland*. It was lodged
" there by Mr. LE CLERC, and it was fent
" to him by the famous Mr. LOCKE, and is
" actually in the hand-writing of this Gen-
" tleman.

" tleman. And notwithstanding the Letters
" have the acknowledged defects, the EDI-
" TOR thought it a pity, that the world
" should be longer deprived of these Two
" Pieces, as they now are, since they cannot
" be obtained more perfect, all other copies
" of them being either lost or destroyed."

F I N I S.

On Friday, April the 5th 1754, will be published,
The ADVENTURER Complete,
In FOUR VOLUMES, *Duodecimo.*
Printed for J PAYNE, at *Pope's-Head,* in *Pater-noster-Row.*

Where may be had,

I. The ADVENTURER, in 2 Vols. Folio, with Contents and Translations. Also, any odd Numbers of the Folio Edition.

II. The Fifth and Sixth Volumes of The RAMBLER, in Duodecimo With Tables of Contents, and a Translation of the Mottos and Quotations for all the Six Volumes.

III. The RAMBLER complete, in Two Volumes Folio, with Contents and Translations, Price only One Pound in Boards.

IV. A Letter from the Lord Archbishop of *Sens,* to Monsieur ******* Counsellor in the Parliament of *Paris.* In Answer to the Parliament's Arret, against the Clergy of *France,* in respect to the Certificates of Confession, and the Bull *Unigenitus.* Translated from the Original *French,* suppressed by the Parliament Price 6 *d.*

V. A Letter to the Archbishop of *Sens,* in Answer to his Lordship's Letter to Monsieur ******* a Counsellor in the Parliament of *Paris.* To which is added, a Copy of the Proceedings of the Parliament of *Paris,* taken from its Registers. Price 1 *s.*

N. B These Two Letters contain a full Account of the present Dispute between the Clergy and Parliament of France.